TAROT
Mirror
of your Relationships

Gerd Ziegler

TAROT

Mirror
of your Relationships

URANIA VERLAGS AG

ISBN 3-908647-03-7

Translator: C. (Shunya) Morgenstern
Production: Schneelöwe, Durach , West Germany

Printed in Germany

Table of Contents

For Navanito

Relationships

Don't hang your heart on anything
live, live totally, live lovingly,
but possess nothing, dominate nothing,
and don't allow
anyone
to possess you
or to dominate you.
Very few, very rare people
rise to the planes of human love.
Human love is friendship.
Animal love is possessive rage.
Animal love reduces the other
to a thing, to a product.
Human love raises the other,
helps the other
to come to his unfolding.
It is pure friendship.

Bhagwan Shree Rajneesh

A partnership has reached its goal when one no longer needs the other. Only in this case the promise of »eternal« love has been put into practice. Love is an act of consciousness, and means opening one's own limits of awareness to that which one loves, in order to become one with it. This has happened only when one has taken into his own all which represents the partner.

Love wants to be one, nothing else. Lucky the person who realizes that the only things which cannot be taken from him are those which he has manifested in himself.

Thorwald Dethlefsen

Foreword and Acknowledgements

I hesitated a long time before I dared write the first pages of this book. I see myself too much as a student in the field of relationships. My publisher had to make a number of attempts before I was willing to engage in a written discussion of this explosive theme. Looking back now on the process of creating this book, I would like to extend my special thanks to him for his »stubbornness«.

Writing this second Tarot book took a good deal more time than writing **Tarot – Mirror of the Soul**. With this book I was much more personally affected by the man-woman theme. I thank all those who were close to me in this time, and gave me the opportunity to experience intimately what I wanted to express in words. The experiences in our time together were a rich source of inspiration for the contents of the Tarot card descriptions.

The many participants in my ongoing Tarot and Training courses are also deserving of special thanks. The openness with which they asked their questions about relationships gave me the opportunity to test the validity of my own experiences. It was a continual gift for all involved to sense and fathom the special depths of their relationships, even when the recongnition of their reality was sometimes painful.

Not least, I wish to thank all those who took the time to look over and criticize my preliminary work, and who helped augment my own descriptions out of their own experiences in Tarot and relations.

Introduction

When I work with the participants in my Tarot workshops on clarifying personal life issues, the majority of the questions asked are about relationships. Questions about career, self expression and personal growth come in second or third.

At first I was astonished that not only current man-woman relationships seemed to be an issue for people, but almost as often distant and unresolved familial questions came up too. Even when the persons's question was directed toward a current relationship, in many cases emotionally loaded early childhood or in some cases karmic memories came up. By looking more precisely at the behavior patterns from the earlier experiences, we were able to see the current problems in a new light. This made free the way to deeper understanding and clarification.

My in-depth work with the psychodynamics of interpersonal relationships taught me quite a bit, as did my own relationships with women, friends, and co-workers. In addition, I learned a lot from my clients and the participants in our training project **(Inwardly and Outwardly Rich)**.

However, that which guides two people together and binds them in love is and remains a mystery. Rational explanations will fortunately never be in a position to tell us. We can come closer to this secret with respect and reverence, in order to use it as a learning process for our own growth. Each of us is deeply affected by the multitudinous aspects of the relationships between man and women, whether we go out of our ways to avoid them or feel driven to seek them. Hidden in our relationships to the people close to us lies the key to the universe. The same door which I open or close to a beloved person is my connection to the Whole, to God, to all which has meaning to me.

For this reason, personal realization and spiritual growth can never slip by without facing the question of relationship. Unresolved areas and situations reach out to hinder and burden us on the way to our personal liberation.

Very often our path to deepest fulfillment – the complete blossoming of our ability to love and receive love – leads us through valleys of disillusionment and purification.

If we are prepared to take the necessary steps in learning both with ourselves and with our partners, our gain can be immeasurable.

To all people who are honestly ready to recognize their relationships as learning processes and aids in their personal and spiritual growth I wish you much insight, many friends, and the blossoming of your universal and infinite love. May this book be an incentive, inspiration and help to all who have the courage to embark on this adventure.

1. Relationship as a Learning Terrain

The possibilities and opportunities to learn and grow through interpersonal relationships are boundless. In order to take full advantage of these opportunities, we have to be prepared to let go all our acquired ideas about how people – especially how men and women – should live and deal with each other. We should accept as a basis for realizing our individual relationships only that which has grown from our own, authentic experience and understanding.

Of course this book springs from my own experiences and insights. If you read it and want to work with it, you will have to judge carefully for yourself whether the instructions and explanations given here correspond and apply ot your own experience.

There really is no »better« or »worse«. We always create exactly the situations in which to learn whatever we need to learn. All the various forms of relationship, including parting and being alone, exist in order to heal and transform us. One way is not better than any other.

When our relationships go through changes, this does not mean that something is wrong. On the contrary, few things are as prone to constant change as are relationships. This has to be the case, because people are themselves continually going through a growth and development process. Living relationships are mutable. They pulsate in a dynamic symphony. If you cling to a certain closeness or distance in a rigid way, the natural flow of love is interrupted. The relationship between intimacy and distance in a relationship is like the process of inhalation and exhalation which keeps every organism alive.

If you look at your life until now, you can see that there have been several people who were, for a period of time, of the utmost importance to you. Yet if you were to compare those connections to your present ones, they have lost that importance to some degree. Perhaps you can remember the pain of parting from someone, and how hard you tried to win them back. Today, looking from a distance, you can see how important that parting was to you. It enabled you to make room in your life for something greater and better.

No relationship falls apart unless there is something more important waiting out there for us. Of course, we can't always recognize this from our limited perspectives. Such situations are a gift given to enable us to experience a greater love. The love we give and receive in relationships is but a reflection of that greater love awaiting us.

2. Letting Yourself Get Involved

I often hear people say »I really wish to have a partner, but whenever someone comes and wants to give me all his love, I get scared and run away.«

Not everyone is aware of this mechanism. Many people just don't allow themselves to get into situations where deep affection might develop. The fact is, we all have that fear to some degree – the fear of being truly loved. Something we yearn for so strongly can frighten and shake us when it breaks into our lives.

For this reason, most people have decided to avoid this alltransforming force. What they call love usually consists of projected fears, needs, expectations, drives, possessiveness, and a desire for power. In this way, it is possible for such people to »give themselves« in a few affairs and adventures without letting themselves be really touched inside. Bored and disappointed, many of them withdraw sooner or later into attitudes of »reasonableness« which are really based only on their resignation and disappointment.

Love is the strongest force in the universe. The more we open ourselves to its energy, the more it transforms all areas of our lives. Love heals, and therefore helps bring to the surface everything which might stand in the way of our realization of our true selves.

When we are well loved by someone, all our inner realms which don't necessarily correspond with this love also come to light. They express themselves often in forms of fear, panic, rage, sadness, jealousy, annoyance and pain. This process starts often during or shortly after the »honeymoon« phase.

It is usually misinterpreted and not understood for what it really is – purification and healing for both partners. In this phase, the high ideals and expectations with which the two came together seem illusionary. Even couples who have great potential together sometimes separate in disappointment with an unexpressed resolve never to open up to love again. They don't want to be disappointed again in such a painful way. Others just grit their teeth and simply reduce the flow affection to a bearable, safe minimum. Both partners stop expecting any fulfillment in their togetherness.

If you want to open yourself to love, you have to realize that every form of love represents a threat to your ego. The ego is the part of our consciousness which experiences itself as separate from the universe. It can only live in duality, in the separation of inside and outside, I and You.

Love, however, wants nothing but to become one. It transcends opposites and brings about the unification of all polarities, creating a new universe within us. We become able to overcome all boundaries. When we have a profound realization and acceptance of the different-ness of our beloved partner, love is born; a love which reveals duality to be an illusion. We become able to recognize those seemingly alien aspects of our partner as our own, latent characteristics. We have no longer any reason to fight them in our partner.

At exactly this point, we suddenly have to deal with fear. We know our true selves so little, how can we know what we will find beyond our egos? We have barely started to allow ourselves into our own insides, how can we do this with another person? We are afraid of losing ourselves, afraid of being thrown forcefully back onto ourselves, afraid to fail again, and to seek in vain the fulfillment we hope to find in our partner.

The path to love will bring us face to face with fear many times. It forces us to see again and again, mercilessly, that nothing of what we seek can be found outside ourselves. It exists only within us. And yet this truth can be made clear to us through our polar opposite outside ourselves, reflecting it back to us. (See also the description of the card »The Lovers«.)

In most love relationships we also confront our own shadowy sides. This can often lead us back to unresolved formative situations in our past. This includes all our primary familial relationships like those with our parents, siblings, grandparents. In addition, our experiences during our gestation and birth and our karma from previous lifetimes have a much greater effect than we may realize. No matter how these difficulties manifest in our present relationships, they always point to old, unhealed wounds. In order to heal them, we must uncover and cleanse them.

Our capacity to love and be loved depends upon willingness and readiness to confront and clear precisely those unpleasant parts of ourselves which we would much rather hide. We can open to other people only to the degree to which we can open ourselves to ourselves.

There can be no true surrender to another person without a simultaneous deep opening to ourselves. If this doesn't happen, the connection to another will be used simply to distract us from ourselves and to attempt to cover up our own inner lackings. We can observe this everywhere in »love relationships« – it seems to be the normal thing to do. But more and more people are becoming ready to dare to take a step beyond, a step to greater responsibility and awareness. In this way they get to know surrender, which always leads in both directions – to ourselves and to the other.

If you break out on this new path, sooner or later you will come upon a new, overwhelming truth. It lies in the realization that there is ultimately only **one** love relationship – the connection between the external personality and the inner being, between my uniqueness and the universal, between the human and the Divine. Our relationships are no more than reflections of this one great relationship. The more this realization grows in us, the more we can see and love our partners as part of our selves. »Getting involved« becomes getting familiar and becoming one with the Divine in us.

3. The Relationship to the Whole

In every relationship with a particular partner we are being directed toward our relationship with the Whole. In deciding to incarnate on the planet Earth as human beings, we have let ourselves in for a learning process whose basic rules are characterized by the illusion of duality.

Duality is manifested in experiencing personal separation from the universal oneness.

Getting cought up in the separation between I and You, between persona and external world, makes possible many consciousness-expanding experiences in our earthly lives. Every time we fall in love, every search for closeness with a partner of the opposite sex is an attempt to transcend the duality in a dyadic experience.

While the most superficial part of ourselves, our ego, experiences itself as absolutely separated from all other people, deep in each indivudual remains the certainty that separation is not the truth. In fact, the word **Individual** means »the indivisible«.

We yearn to regain our cosmic oneness from which we came. This desire is what fuels our search for the other. At the same time it is the ground for many misunderstandings in human relationships. This happens because the natural desire for oneness can never be fully satisfied in the long run in the relationship to another person. Union with the beloved repeatedly promises an end to separation. The more intelligent a person is, the more quickly he or she will sense that the connection to the Whole is not to be found in another separate part. Immature people tend to make their partners responsible, at this point, for their disappointment. They heap bitter accusations upon their partners, or leave them in order to repeat the same experience with the next partner.

What we seek is oneness with our divine core, with our »higher selves«. This is why we can only temporarily find an end to our separateness with another person. We are thrown back on ourselves again and again until we realize that the source of the experience of oneness is to be found only in ourselves.

Often, people lock themselves into a couple-relationship and then experience even more clearly their separation from those around them. The couple becomes a unit, sometimes a fortress. As a result, a chasm forms between the intimacy the two experience in their relationship, and the so-called outside world, which appears more and more alien and threatening to the couple. This is a clear example of how illusory oneness which two people want to keep up together, leads in time to separation from the life around them. What a bitter realization it is for many, when they see that their efforts to find union with a beloved person has actually led to a new form of isolation. When this happens, most people choose, either consciously or unconsciously, that this is the time to end the relationship. Somehow they feel that the relationship doesn't give them what they really want – union with their true selves.

Our love should become a gateway, an entrance, a passage, an initiation into the experience of cosmic oneness. When we learn to see our relationships from this perspective, the closeness we achieve with one another takes on something real and deep. We experience a new sort of freedom in realizing that oneness with the Whole does not necessarily require relationships. They can be a key, an aid, but they are not a goal in themselves. Once we understand this, all our relationships can become enriching, because they are in harmony with universal truth.

4. Practical Hints for Using this Book

Relationships are usually extremely complex and multilayered. You may find yourself in a situation argument with your partner in which neither of you really know what is going on. You feel touched or bored, pressured or relieved, scared or impatient, overwhelmed or ignored, loved or deserted by your partner's closeness.

What is the deeper reality of this interaction in which so much unawareness and irrationality is rampant. What unknown forces are at work? Why did the existence bring me together with this particular person whose presence is having such a great impact on my life? Can I trust my own feelings and perceptions and those of my partner?

These and similar questions concern us again and again, and our limited intellect can never answer them satisfactorily.

Tarot can grant us insights which take us beyond the boundaries of our limited points of view. By allowing our intuition to function, we can come into contact in a meditative way with our inner wisdom. Through the power source of our subconscious we arrive at a connection to our »higher selves«. The cards themselves have no answers to our questions. They merely serve as an aid to help us to more easily recognize and understand the messages and signals we are sending ourselves.

Before taking this book and the cards into your hands to ask the questions about your relationship that concern you, you should take time to get in touch with this inner authority. Sit quietly and comfortably, open yourself, and wait until your breath flows softly and deeply. Listen inward, and observe everything that happens in your thoughts and feelings. Be aware that you are in the process of looking into the mirror of a deeper reality. Be open when your draw a card to any and all possible answers which the image could show you. As your openness increases, so does your trust in your intuition, the contact to your »higher self«.

Each card is discussed in regard to the following questions:

»What is the present reality in my relationship concerning... «

»What ist the basic energy characterizing the current situation between me and my partner?«

»What areas of my relationship need special attention?«

The texts are geared toward the theme of relationships between men and women. I have assumed that the reader is familiar with the descriptions of the symbols and their basic meanings as laid out in **Tarot, Mirror of the Soul**. This will avoid unnecessary repetitions.

If you want to learn more about other, non-sexual relationships such as those between you and your child(ren), parents, friends or colleagues, look for the more generalized and basic content of the card you draw, and then try to apply the essence of the text to that relationship.

You can also use the texts in another way. At a quiet time, for example, just before going to sleep, with or without your partner, draw a card from the fanned-out deck. If you are with your partner, read each other the text about the card you have drawn. In this way you can take an important aspect of the relationship with you into sleep, so that your subconscious can work on it further. This will soon help intensify and deepen your relationship.

If you are presently living alone and are looking for a fulfilling partnership, you should practise the above-mentioned method as well over a period of time. In this way you can confront the partner you hope for as if he or she were already there. We know that the power of our thoughts and imaginations is infinitely creative. The themes and ideas with which we concern ourselves intensely tend to manifest in our lives. Even encounters with imaginary partners prepare us internally to meet him or her at some later time in reality.

24

5. Interpretations of the Cards

A. The Major Arcana (0–XXI)

0. The Fool

Key Words: *Freedom, openess, readiness to take risks; trust; surrender; humor, wisdom, courage; overcoming fear; quantum leap, finding yourself; a life oriented toward love.*

The Fool is an emphatic invitation to engage in a real love adventure. When you draw this card in regard to a beloved person, you are being challenged to try something out of the ordinary – to take a leap into the uncertainty and freedom which lies beyond all that you already know and do.

The rational mind calculates, reckons, and protects itself. The Fool, on the other hand, unerringly follows his own inner reality. He shows us an unequivocal »yes« to the call of the heart. Only by saying that »yes« we can take the leap into love which is, at the same time, an inner quantum leap toward our own transformations and our liberation from fear.

When you draw The Fool, it indicates that three themes are of importance now in your relationship. They are openness, freedom and willingness to take risks. Fools wear their hearts on their sleeves, which can be both foolish and dangerous in »normal« everyday life. But a relationship with a person who is close to you can develop in value and worth only when you can be open and say things without first calculating their effect. Being open means – showing, with or without words, all which is within you. Oppenness also means, however, the willingness on your part to receive all which your partner will give; the love as well as the pain, the tenderness as well as the sorrow. And last, but not least, openness means listening to the voice of your heart and going with what is there, even if it is different than what you had imagined.

When there is complete openness between you and your partner, freedom develops all by itself. The essence of freedom, represented by The Fool, is the ability to leave behind you all ideals, norms, and obligations set by those outside you. In a relationship this means that you don't orient yourself by what you have learned from parents and teachers about the meanings of togetherness, marriage and family. The reality of the moment between you and your partner is so unique that no value systems based on ideologies can do justice to it. Freedom means that you remain unfailingly loyal to your own inner reality. The Fool is prepared to walk the path of the heart, which is oriented by love, not fear.

Fear is freedom's greatest enemy. The Fool is attacked repeatedly by the Tiger of Fear, but never lets himself be overwhelmed. You can feel your fear, accept it, and still keep on your own unmistakable path.

If you don't let fear hold you back, you are risking a lot. For example, if the Fool has a choice between two possible partners, he will not choose the one who offers him the greatest security. He lets himself be guided by his heart, his inner voice and goes where he feels himself most strongly pulled. And if he is most strongly pulled to two people, he goes to both. He may soon be left standing alone again, but even that won't shake his trust in himself and his heart. Deep inside, the Fool knows that whatever happens is always exactly what he needs for his own inner growth and personal development. The less he resists and defends himself against it, the easier this growth will be. The Fool does not choose the comfortable way at any price. Everyone who lives a life based on self-trust rather than security and accomodation sooner or later comes face to face with the fundamental insecureness of existence. If you surrender and give yourself fully to life or to a beloved person, you leave the safe shores of your well-known and well-ordered world and find new qualities of caring and protection in yourself and in the Whole.

Question: *Where is your heart calling you to go?*

Suggestion: *Examine in which areas of your life or relationship you don't yet dare to stand by yourself.*

Affirmation: *I follow the voice of my heart.*

I. The Magus

Key Words: *Easy, open communication; powerfull aura; wit; merriment; play; exchange on many levels; vitality; openness; amorality; mobility.*

Many levels of exchange are open now between you an your partner, and you can get to know them all easily and playfully. Enjoy exploring the many different variations of communication and togetherness!

When you draw this card for questions about your relationship, it shows that you are in a phase of being able to »enchant« others in the truest meaning of the word. Other people besides your partner are interested in you. Don't avoid them.

A person who is living in a happy relationship also has an attracting effect on ohters. Your partner probably has a strong influence on your fascinating aura. If you feel very good together, you can easily experience the many different forms of interchange both inside and outside of your relationship. You can have fun learning to combine and connect your relationship and the »outer« world.

This card can also mean that your behavior is causing all old ideas and principles which once were valid between you and your partner to be called into question and thoroughly examined. If this is the case, you will have to be careful to incorporate all provocations and conflicts into your striving toward more openess and real-ness in your relationship; put conflict to work in the service of love. The all-too serious aspects of your partnership can well be set aside for a while. You can experience your relationship as part of the great cosmic game. The easiness and lightness of your interchange does not in any way indicate superficialitiy. You can still touch on inner realism which our usual dry and serious social manners can never reach. If your partner reacts to your vitality with fear or rejection, don't be fooled – your openness will likely rub off on him or her soon.

This card indicates that there are »divine messages« to be received in your relationship. Pass these on to other people. The Magus can also indicate a project in the area of communication which you will take on together. By fully expressing the creative potential of your relationship, you will find yourself even happier and more fulfilled. Find fitting ways to let others have a part in your love.

Here we should also discuss the two other designs Frieda Harris created for the Magus. In the new edition of the cards, they are included as extra cards (unfortunately and this means the black and white cards have been ommitted in the new decks.) The pictures are portrayals of the white and the black Magus. The following is for those who want to include these two cards in their decks.

The **white Magus** serves all that is good, positive, light, radiant. He is completely aligned with this pole of the duality. He is recognized by the winged symbol of the sun above his head. The powerful serpent in the background indicates that his kundalini energy is integrated on all levels and is in harmony with the whole.

In your relationship, this Magus means that mostly light and clear forces are at work. Your communication is open, clear and honest.

The **black Magus** has a winged symbol of the sun and the kundalini in the lower energy centers. Whether he is aware or not, his actions serve darker forces, represented by the demonic monster in the background. This magician uses his powers selfishly to his own ends, thereby setting himself against the will of the whole.

In regard to your relationship this card shows a present tendency to use others, or misuse them, for your own purposes. You may use pressure or seduction to possess and make a dependent creature of your partner. Your partner is a means to satisfy your expectations and demands. If he or she fails to do so, punishment will be meted out.

The Magus which Crowley authorized to be used in his Tarot can be seen as the **transcendent Magus**. He carries the forces of both light and darkness, which gives him a shimmering glow. This magician knows both poles and has integrated them. The winged sun is high over his head. He is beyond morals and can use either dark or light energies for his work toward transcendence. He knows that ultimately all and everything is part of the Whole; and everything helps make possible our quantum leap out of duality. Freedom exists beyond both good and bad. From this perspective, the wise one sees that everything is part of the same cosmic game.

Everything mentioned earlier in this explanation applies mostly to the transcendent Magus and in part to the white one.

Question: *What areas of your relationship would you like to discuss and explore with your partner more fully?*

Suggestion: *Meditate on the statement, »If you want to experience magic, let your armor fall. Magic is stronger than steel.« (from* **Bridge Through Time** *by Richard Beach).*

Affirmation: *I communicate openly, easily and freely.*

II. The Priestess

Key Words: *Soulmates, spiritual relationship; possibility of recognizing the »higher« purpose; familiarity, connectedness, intuition; independence, freedom; contact to the »higher self«; integration of the inner male and female aspects.*

The Priestess emphasizes the spiritual aspect of a relationship. She embodies the connection to infinity; she is an image of the non-material, the light beyond light and darkness.

You feel a deep spiritual relationship with your partner, you are soul-mates and some special task has led you together. The

30

part inside you which is of the opposite sex no longer needs to be projected onto the partner outside you. As you develop this aspect of yourself, wisdom and freedom will grow, until you are able to accept your partner and face your partner as a complete and whole individual. Your relationship needs no longer be characterised by neediness. What you share with each other arises from your inner wealth, your personal experience. This lends your interaction a ripeness and maturity which can lead you to new planes of togetherness.

Even if your relationship is beset by difficult problems, you can still feel a connection between you which is not limited to time and space. Even if the sexual attraction between you diminishes, the subtle and fine energy lines connecting you remain strong.

You are possibly not even aware of the »higher« planes of your relationship to their full extent. But now is a good time to open yourself to those dimensions and recognize their value. Allow minor conflicts between you to fade into the background. Your connection is so strong, you can let yourselves focus on your individuality (»indivisibility«) and independence.

Open yourself to free and harmonious giving and receiving. Be open to relationships with other people. Accept the fact that what binds you together is not passion as much as something much more cosmic in nature. The still, unspeakable knowledge of your connectedness can lead you into deeper realms than any physical orgasm could.

Freedom and friendship are coming to the forefront now. The freedom you give your partner is rooted in your own sense of fulfillment, your own ability to integrate the feminine and masculine aspects of your nature. If you feel the need to take space and time for yourself now, this arises from deep part of yourself. In no way it sacrifices your sense of togetherness with your partner. In fact, you are able, in your temporary alone-ness, to generate new energy and inner wisdom which you will be able to share fruitfully with your partner. By allowing freedom you can become more free, and your sense of freedom will encompass and enrich your relationship.

The Priestess also indicates that you can help each other develop your intuitive abilities. You may even develop a joint project as a result of this work. In any case you are both in positions to help each other come into closer contact with your inner guides and healers. Even if you are separated by great distances, you can remain in telepathic contact.

Question: *To which people do you feel a special connectedness on higher planes?*

Suggestion: *Meditate regularly with your partner.*

Affirmation: *I trust my intuitive wisdom and share it with people who are open to it.*

III. The Empress

Key Words: *Anima; femininity, beauty, harmony, love, abundance; motherliness, vital emotionality, sensitivity.*

The Empress represents Woman. She embodies the quality of the female prinicple (Yin), the opposite of the male principle (Yang). Her distinctive characteristics are receptivity, abundance, beauty, nourishing, fertility, form-giving, surrender, flowing, and empathy.

In regard to questions about relationship, the card indicates qualities of beauty, strength, aesthetics, wealth, wisdom and abundance in your partnership.

When a woman draws this card, she is being shown her opportunity to develop her own femininity at her partner's side. She can sense that her empathy and receptivity are neither weakness nor a sign of submission but the expressions of special strength. Her emotionality is not moodiness but lively vitality, and her motherliness is not possessiveness but true strength and the expression of a warm heart. When a woman is true to herself as a woman (and each woman must know for herself which qualities express her femininity), she is not only attractive and enticing to her partner but can also help him to develop and fully express the man within him.

If you draw this card, you are committed to making your relationship a place for rejoicing, enjoyment, loveliness, beauty and love. You are mother and goddess, beloved and queen, Empress and wise woman. Your extraordinary radiance invites your partner and others into your sphere to spend time sharing the harmony of your being.

You have drawn this card because you are able to get in touch with all these qualities and are ready to deal with your woman-ness on much deeper levels.

When a man draws this card, the message is that his partner now is his ideal female counterpart. Everything he seeks in a woman is available in his present partner. He should recognize her as his teacher. He can receive from her many things which relate to his own feminine side (the anima, the woman within). By entering into closeness and intimacy, he can allow her to help him integrate the other side of himself which he has repressed or neglected; she shows him his sensitivity, vulnerability, tenderness, emotionality, ability to surrender and his grace.

If your relationship is full of conflict or you are afraid of »too much« closeness, this card is showing you the necessity and opportunity of dealing with and resolving unclarified aspects of your relationship with your mother. You may feel hemmed in or stifled by your partner, or you may yearn in vain for warmth and security; you may be struggling for recognition and love, or feel overwhelmed by your partner's desires and needs. If any of these are the case and you have drawn the Empress in regard to the situation, her message to you is that the struggles you are engaged in are no more than shadow-boxing matches. You are ready and able now to recognize those out-dated mother-projections and cease engaging in them. As you gain access and closeness to your woman within, old fears will drop away and you will be able to see your partner for what she really is.

Question: *What are the qualities of your woman within?*

Suggestion: *Yin-Yang game: Give yourselves a good amount of time to be together. You will take turns playing the roles of the feminine and the masculine aspects or principles. For example, you may be the masculine or active aspect for one day and your partner will be the feminine or receptive aspect. Then you can change roles. Before and again after playing this game, discuss how you understand and experienced the two roles.*

Affirmation: *I develop my feminine portion and express it.*

IV. The Emperor

Key Words: *Animus; maleness; authority; father, power; the male aspects of man and woman.*

The Emperor represents the man in relationships. He embodies the quality of the male principle (Yang) as the belance to the female principle (Yin). His characteristics are the active, form- and structure-giving, the fiery and dynamic, the penetrating and conquering, the will, directness, action, and force.

If we apply these qualities to human relationship, the Emperor represents male autority, fatherliness, the one who masters and forms matter, the initiator, and the leader.

In a society which has a one-sided slant toward the male aspect, a society like the western one we live in, these principles become rigid. They have taken on extreme and perverse forms. The average »man of character« becomes more or less a victim of social role-ideals. These ideals force him to deny and fight against the feminine aspects, the female parts of himself. This

34

gives rise to authoritarianism, the need to control himself which becomes a caricature of true male virtues. The more a man rejects his inner feminine aspect, the more he tends to oppress the real women around him.

Both aspects – true manliness and rigid role-playing – are spoken to by this Tarot card. When a man draws this card, he is being encouraged to recognize the realms of his male power and express them intrepidly. You can develop your masculine aspects at your partner's side.

It is important, especially at this moment, for you to liberate yourself from your old, conditioned ideas about your masculinity. If you don't, you run the risk of confusing true strength with rigid, authoritarian behavior. You should avoid building up power positions which make you inaccessible to others. By showing your softness and sensitivity, your weakness, and neediness, you develop your true greatness as a man. That greatness allows you to be whole and complete. If you develop and allow your real masculinity in your relationship, you allow your partner to develop her own true femininity.

If a woman draws this card, she is being asked to confront her own masculine side to get to know it and develop it. Your husband, friend, or lover (or even a boss or another male authority figure) takes on the function of bringing you into contact with your own inner masculine aspect. If this man attracts you, he represents important aspects of your animus, your inner man. What attracts you to men outside yourself are your own inner qualities which are seeking development, expression, and fulfillment.

If your relationship is full of conflict, now is probably the time for you to face and work with unresolved and troublesome areas connected with your father. You yearn for a man with real strength at whose side you can develop your own feminine aspect. You desire deep surrender, so you make certain demands on your partner which he may be completely unable to satisfy. As long as you seek in men a perfect father or your own un-realized and undeveloped animus or male aspect, your relationships with men will be characterized by struggles against your partner's inaccessiblity or unavailability.

Question: *What are the qualities of your inner man?*

Suggestion: *Yin-Yang Game (described under III. The Empress).*

Affirmation: *I develop and give expression to my male aspects.*

V. The High Priest (The Hierophant)

Key Words: *Spirituality; search for the inner guide or teacher; wisdom; meditation; soul mates; readiness to learn from one another; shared process of learning and becoming conscious.*

Like The High Priestess, the Hierophant brings the spiritual aspects of your relationship to the forefront. More important than your sexual male-female connection is your knowledge of the soul-mate natur of your relationship. This is totally independent of any incidental and transitory love affairs.

Your partner is not only your friend or lover, but in a certain sense also your teacher and guide. If you can recognize and accept this, you will face him or her in a different way in both your daily encounters and in moments of conflict and controversy. This does not mean you should start looking up to your partner, as if you can only learn from someone you are submissive to. In love there is only equality – equal giving and receiving. Every soul has as much to learn as the other has to teach. So be sure to view your partner as an equal, even when you are learning from and with him or her.

If you can grant another person a »teaching role« in your life, this is a sign of your intelligence, your understanding, and your maturity. Your companion can help you to get in touch with your own inner guide. This happens in a natural way, just through the special quality of the bonds which connect you.

Very often, however, relationships seem to evolve into a

one-sided situation with one partner as the superior »teacher« and the other as the awed »pupil«. Such a relationship breaks down the moment the »pupil« becomes independent or the »teacher« finds the role too burdensome. These patterns can be called neurotic. People entangled in such situations rarely draw The Hierophant. If someone in such a relationship should draw this card, the message to the »teacher« is to open your eyes and see that you, in fact, have a great deal to learn and receive from your partner. If you are the »pupil« in the relationship, the message is to become aware in which areas of your life you recognize your partner as a teacher and in which you do not. Talk openly with your partner about this.

Role playing like this is often based on unconscious and unspoken agreements. The more consciously you deal with this, the faster you can free your relationship of neurotic ballast. You will then be able to move forward more directly and quickly into the deeper levels of your Hierophant-ic connection. You may be one of the few lucky couples who succeed in bringing your routine day-to-day life into close harmony with your shared spiritual work.

In any case, the Hierophant is telling you that important learning and consciousness-expanding processes are taking place in your relationship with this partner. The sexual aspect may become a background issue as time goes on. But be aware that the companionship you share on your spiritual search binds you in a way we can call timeless.

Your connection with your partner is most likely a longstanding one. You probably felt familiar with each other right away when you met, and maybe you felt »We already know each other«. Even if you did not meet in earlier lives, you both carry ancient wisdom within you can now call awake in each other. The most important thing the two of you can do right now is to meditate together. This card is also a hint that other spiritual relationships are also important for you. They may involve people who, for some »mysterious« reason, fascinate you or a spiritual master whose presence you should seek. Certain books may have a meaningful role to play for you now.

The most important spiritual relationship you can experience, however, is the one with your own inner »higher self« or guide. When you draw the Hierophant, your inner guide is knocking at your door somehow. Find out how to meet this guide more often and more deeply.

Question: *Are you ready to learn from your partner?*

Suggestion: *Tell each other in which areas you can learn from each other.*

Affirmation: *In being with my partner I discover myself.*

VI. The Lovers

Key Words: *Love; relationship as learning tool; striving for oneness; meeting of opposites; intensity; completeness; transcendence.*

»The Lovers« is definitely **the** central card in relationship Tarot. Like no other card in the deck, it shows the desire, the attraction, the conflict, and the adventure of the striving for union of those opposite poles, man and woman.

Many myths in various cultures tell of the original division of the sexes – the fall from original oneness. These memories seem to be deeply rooted in the human collective unconscious. They all tell that man and woman were created as a single unit. Only later were they divided into two.

»When the nature of humanity was split, each half yearned for the other and bound itself with the other; they wound their arms around each other, they clung to each other in their need to melt together as one . . . Thus the love for one's neighbour was instilled in a distant time; the love which unifies us with our original nature; the love that attempts to make from two beings a single being, in other words, to heal our nature!«

(from Plato, Symposium)

The cosmic experiment with duality on this planet prevents the direct path which leads back to our original dream-like unity from opening to us. This unity may have been a heavenly condition of total bliss, but the individual in a state of pre-conscious being could not recognize it as such. The fish in an ocean does not know that its life is spent in water. Only when it is torn from its original oneness, it can realize consciously what it has taken for granted. Separated from its nourishing, essential element, struggling on a sand bank, its entire being yearns for reunion.

Duality makes our fall from cosmic oneness visible and perceptible. Our desperate yearning to end the separation and become one with the beloved expresses our desire for union with the cosmic ocean. Our attempts, however, repeatedly reveal themselves to be illusions as long as we seek that union in an external partner, demanding that he or she should be the one to make us whole.

»As long as we seek our sexual wholeness outside ourselves, we will inevitably experience a painful lack and terrifying chasm which we attempt to bridge with an intense and full emotional and love life, yet our attempts are in vain. We know very well that in all emotional relationships the fear of losing the beloved person can lead to unrest and worry... Every passionate feeling which is centered on a particular individual must be equated with tension and disturbance.«

(Cecile Sagne, **Geheiligter Eros**, Heyne pub. Munich 1987)

This vicious circle of illusions can only be escaped when we realize on much deeper levels that the oneness and complation we seek can be found and created only **within** each of us. Every man and every woman contains the two polar opposites (Anima and Animus) within. A liberated person has united these male and female natures within; anima and animus are reconciled, the opposite poles are integrated, and thus duality is overcome.

The Lovers indicates that you can now achieve a taste of that ultimate oneness in your relationship with your beloved partner. Your relationship is an invaluable space for you to learn and experiment. You can experience directly what has to develop within you in order to realize your wholeness for you.

Love is not a problem to be solved, but a mystery to be **lived**. If you have drawn this card in relation to your partner, it indicates you have an opportunity to experience and savor everything that is possible between two people who truly love each other. Your relationship can open dimensions for both of you which you would never be able to experience on your own.

The more you let yourself go in love, the richer your life will be. This does not necessarily mean you will experience only the tender and pleasurable aspect of love; you will also need to be open to its darker side – jealousy, conflict, pain, parting. Don't try to avoid conflicts with your partner. If they are there, go into them deeply. When you accept and understand differences you will slowly become able to let go of your demands, expectations and projections and see your partner as he or she really is. Your partner is not the manifestation of what you are missing, but an individual who is infinitely different from you. Only when you create free space for your partner **not** to belong to you in any way you can accept his or her reality in whatever form it manifests. When you are able to perceive your partner's uniqueness, you will constantly feel thrown back on yourself, which will help you recognize your own completeness and resolve your feelings of being split or divided.

Question: *What does your partner give you which you feel you lack inside yourself?*

Suggestion: *If the above explanation seems too complicated and difficult to understand, let it go for now. Just dive headfirst into the challenges of your love relationship. After a while you can re-read the thoughts above. Maybe you will understand them better then!*

Affirmation: *Love is not a problem to be solved but a mystery to be lived.*

VII. The Chariot

Key Words: *New beginning; time of preparation and clarification; meditation; looking inward; journey into expanded realms of being.*

For you and therefore also for your relationship, a new beginning of a fundamental nature is on its way. It will involve entering into expanded realms of being. You may already see clearly where these changes are leading. Your life itself is setting out clear signs and signals indicating the coming change. You might, however, only have an inkling, an inexplicable feeling that your present situation will not remain the same for long. The Chariot usually signals not only inner transformation, but also eventual visible expansion in your style of living.

You are choosing a new path and the first question to clarify before starting out is »Its this way also my partner's way?« If your partner is trying to hinder or restrain you in any way, go on without him. If, however, your partner is headed in the same direction, now is the time for the two of you to make all necessary preparations both internally and externally for your shared journey.

What will this preparation look like? If you look carefully at the card, you will see that the Chariot driver is meditating. The spinning disk symbolizes the wheel of fortune, and the driver's gaze indicates his meditative inward concentration. In deep meditation he considers and examines all possible consequences of his start into a broadened future.

Meditation done together is one possible way of preparing yourselves mentally and spiritually. You also need to prepare for your new beginning on the material plane. This means you need to have clarity in your living situation, your career, and your finances. Conditions and situations need to be cleansed and clarified in order to allow old phases to be resolved and closed.

The Chariot often indicates imminent projects which you could do well if you take them on, either alone or together. These projects may involve your profession or your home and family life. In any case, such large undertakings will influence and redefine your relationship. Remember to be inwardly prepared for what is coming.

You will be able to complete many of the preparations together, but some you will have to do alone. Perhaps one or both of you will need a certain amont of time and space to be alone. If this is the case, be sure to stand by your need to be alone, and respect your partner's need to withdraw temporarily. When all is done, start without fear. Your chances are very good, even if the »journey« ends up looking less predictable and smooth than you had imagined. Set your goals but be prepared for surprises. The expansion of your lives and ways of being is sure to explode through the boundaries of your imagination.

Question: *What areas of your life are the targets of this new beginning? What consequences do you see in these changes for your relationship?*

Suggestion: *Make an accounting of your present living situation. Each of you is to draw up a list using these words as cues for evaluation: Living situation, career, creative expression (hobby, etc.), body, money, relationship to my partner, other relationships, sexuality. For each cue word, describe the present situation, dividing your impressions into what is negative and what is positive. At the end, formulate the desires or goals open to you in each area. Then discuss your lists and choose the areas in which change is most important for you. Formulate positive affirmations for your desired changes, and work consistently* *with them. Consider what concrete steps you can take to come closer to your goal.*

Affirmation: *I am organizing my life and preparing for the new beginning.*

VIII. Adjustment

Key Words: *Meditation; harmony, balance, inner equilibrium; centeredness; at rest in your own center; clarity; oneness.*

The zodiac sign Libra, which this card is based on, stands for, among other things, the realms of partnersphip, marriage, or similar relationships. When you draw this card, it is speaking to these aspects of your present situation with your partner. You may be experiencing the balance and centeredness depicted on this card. Even if you aren't, your drawing this card indicates your readiness for a harmonious relationship. You yearn for clarity and true inner peace, and you are ready to exert yourself toward attaining them. Just be sure that your efforts toward harmony and regulated circumstances are not an expression of any fear of openness and spontaneity.

This card applies to the inner as well as the outer. Many relationships wither and fade internally because the partners take on the impossible attempt to secure the love they feel for each other through marriage, or judicial, or personal contracts. Love is a child of freedom! If you try to chain and lock it up, the first step is taken toward destroying it.

The depths of your connection to each other has nothing to do with security. If you get to know love and meditation, you have no need to replace or' secure what you have experienced in the depths of your being through external formalities.

The balance and harmony shown in this card arise from a deep inner experience, from a state of being, which of course is also manifested externally. This equilibrium has a quality of meditative being. It comes from finding and accepting your own center, and does not need to be propped up with the crutches of formalities and contracts.

This card does not always indicate existing harmony and balance. It can also mean that the present situation in your relationship is jeopardizing your own inner stability. Your relationship may have been put to the test through some difficult circumstances. You are confronted with insecurity, experience shattering conflicts and feel you are thrown far from your own center. You balance on a tiny point, like the point of the sword on the card, and seek vainly for some sure and steady hold.

Adjustment is not a card of confrontation. If there are problems now between you and your partner and you draw this card, it means »Retreat for a while, meditate each alone and then come together again. Distance and clarity gained through meditation can make your openness deeper and more fruitful«.

Basically, you can understand this card as an invitation to find your point of balance between the poles, between nearness and distance, giving and taking, yin und yang. All forms of physical or emotional disturbance are given us in order to throw us back on ourselves and guide us toward more meditation. Even the present situation of your realtionship is serving your inner purification and cleansing. You need to realize that after a certain point in your personal growth, the practice of meditation ceases to be a luxury and becomes a necessity.

Relationships don't exist to function well. They serve the purpose of supporting us in unfolding and developing to our greatest potential. The ultimate point in this process is the realization that diving into our own centers is the same as regaining our cosmic oneness.

If you experience your relationship with your partner as very mature and highly developed already, use this opportunity to dive together into new depths. Take time for meditation together or perform rituals together. Let yourselves find your centers again and again, and be carried into the worlds beyond the rational mind.

Question: *In what way does your partner help you find your center?*

Suggestion: *Sit together and light a candle in front of you. Look at the flame for half an hour without moving your eyelids. If your eyes tear, let them and keep looking at the flame. Put your consciousness into the center of the flame. When you close your eyes again, let the light of the flame continue to burn in your hearts and spread out.*

Affirmation: *My relationship with my partner helps me discover my inner center.*

IX. The Hermit

Key Words: *Finding your own inner light; self-exploration; withdrawing, being alone; possible parting; integrating the shadow aspect.*

The primary theme in your life revolves around your search for your own inner light. Look closely to see if your present relationship supports this goal.

In the midst of deep involvement with another person, you may be feeling thrown back on yourself. Shadowy aspects of yourself may be coming to the surface, and you sense that you can no longer avoid dealing with them. Now is the time for you to turn your attention completely inward. This may come about through conflicts with a person who is important to you, or through your leaving someone, or being left yourself. Half-hearted or superficial relationships are no longer satisfying.

This phase will bring you into contact, at least temporarily, with your existential loneliness. This is a fundamental aspect of our human existence. We all enter this life alone and we leave it alone. In the short span of time between birth and death, we spend much of our energies in trying to deny our loneliness by seeking out togetherness with ohters. When our diversions and attempts to escape the facts finally fail and we are confronted with our true loneliness, shock and panic may be our first reactions.

You will perceive this state as hopeless, miserable loneliness as long as you feel you are deficient or inwardly lacking. You may feel you are missing something, you can't stop thinking about your partner, your need and desire for him or her may gnaw at you and consume whatever joy you might have felt in life. Only when you allow yourself to fall totally into these tortuous realms of your inner being you can find your true self, your inner light. The moment you arrive there, your loneliness becomes an ecstatic experience of your true being alone – being »all-one«.

Only when you have come to know these inner realms you will be ready for a mature relationship. You will no longer blindly project all the pain which comes from separate being onto your partner and/or the outside world. You will learn to turn those energies inward to serve your own tranformation process.

This Tarot card shows that you need to work with your old shadows so that you can receive new things in your life. The card may also indicate temporary or final partings. In any case, you should allow yourself and your partner plenty of space to withdraw and explore your selves. In doing so, you will find that the fulfillment you hoped to achieve by your partner can only be found in yourself.

Others may help you find the key to your inner self. But if your relationship does not serve this purpose, you are better off ending it. Despite the pain of parting, you will feel real and well in your loneliness.

Question: *Does your relationship serve your inner growth?*

Suggestion: *Read again the section called, »The Relationship to the Whole«.*

Affirmation: *Through being alone I experience being All-One.*

X. Fortune

Key Words: *Great fortune; positive turning point in the relationship; fortunate and happy new beginning; expansion; enrichment; broadening.*

The great good fortune you have wished for so long is now upon you. Either there will be a fortunate turning point in your relationship, or you are in the process of getting to meet the partner of your dreams. In any case, prepare yourself for a tremendous, fortunate broadening and expansion in your love life.

In order for this expansion to take place, you must now be ready to let go of old, restrictive structures. The great and the new just won't fit into your narrow old cubby-holes sharped by thoughts of security and limited belief systems. You have overlooked your own worth long enough, you have covered your own value with self-doubts long enough. Now is the time to learn to love yourself, to recognize and acknowledge yourself, and to accept the external gifts coming to you through your partner. These gifts are merely a reflection of your own inner richness.

You and your beloved are going through a time of great intensity. There is so much going on right now, be generous enough to let the little things slide. And don't resist all the changes going on inside and outside you. Everything that is changing now is for your advantage and will enrich you!

You can view your good fortune as a gift of your growth. This gift is greater than your ego – it is not something you have earned in any way. And when it leaves again, don't try to cling to it. Sooner or later you will understand that true fortune and true happiness is an inner quality which is independent of all external changes.

This fortune which is coming into your life through a beloved person is a hint of the inner bliss you contain – that bliss is your ultimate goal.

Question: *What does Fortune mean to you in relation to your partner?*

Suggestion: *Become aware of the fortune which has come into your life through your partner. Show it to your partner in love and thankfulness.*

Affirmation: *The fortune I experience through others leads me to my inner fulfillment.*

XI. Lust

Key Words: *Lust; overcoming confining moral codes; honesty; joy in life; physicality; passion; sensuality; renewal; sexuality; integrating the shadows; ecstasy; taming the inner beast.*

Live out your lust – that, in short, is the message of this card. Live out your lust – it sounds so simple, yet for most of us it is so difficult to do really.

Lust or pleasure, has to be savored, tasted, and imbibed fully if we want to discover its valuable creative potential. This potential is found by discovering, accepting, understanding, and integrating our animal nature; our drives, passions, wildness, aggressiveness. If we free all those energies which slumber in our »beast« and tame them, we can acquire this tremendous transforming potential.

Our upbringing and repressive moral codes have taught us to fight our drives and »shadowy sides«. But repression prevents our integrating or making them our own – instead, we feel split. Thus we lose our connection to the source of our joy in living.

You now have a great opportunity in your relationship – you can let go of all guilt feelings, old moral standards, and tabus in order to make space for something new – transformation. You can live out your lust if you are ready to surrender and to be honest. Surrender means above all to let yourself fall, to follow all the impulses of your body and let yourself be led by them. Let happen whatever will happen. Honesty means showing your partner your inclinations and needs. Tell her or him what you like, express what is happening in you, what you feel is lacking for you and what could help you to live out and fully enjoy your lust. Experiment with each other! Allow your wildness and craziness free rein!

In this manner, you will come upon your shadowy sides sooner or later. These are all the aspects of yourself which you are afraid of, which scare you, which somehow go beyond your usual good and careful behavior. Be aware that these are important sides of yourselves which you have to get to know in order to become whole. You will need courage, energy, and uncompromising honesty. Live it all out, but do so with full awareness; ride the beast but don't let it ride you! The reins are in your hands.

The lust you experience is by no means to physical pleasure. It can also be love of life which permeates all realms of your existence.

While this card is an invitation to pleasure, it is also a warning at the same time, not to lose yourself in pleasure. Lust is no more than a passing stage. Don't allow it to become an end in itself. The energies set free by your lust should, after a time, be offered to the purifying fire to be illuminated and transformed. In this way, sexual ecstasy can become a cosmic experience and passion can become boundless universal love.

Question: *In which areas do you find it easy and in which do you find it difficult to show your animal natur?*

Suggestion: *The next time you are intimate with your partner, share all your erotic fantasies and sexual desires. Say everything* *you never dared to wish for aloud before. Then let your partner share with you...*

Affirmation: *By accepting and expressing my lust with awareness, I become whole and complete.*

XII. The Hanged Man

Key Words: *Stalled or stagnant relationship; rigidity; helplessness; surrender; letting go.*

Your relationship is at a dead end. The interchange of feelings has ceased. Your efforts to revitalize your love only make the recognition of this blockage more painful. What was once a well-spring of joy, pleasure, and inspiration is now frozen. You try bitterly to defend your stance, only to note again and again that the other simply does not understand you. You each hold to your positions and are not willing to give even an inch.

What can you do to overcome this stuckness? First you must recognize your own helplessness. All forms of defense and struggle pull you down deeper, just as the struggles of a person in quicksand hasten his demise.

The helplessness confronting you now is of an existential nature – you are confronting a basic aspect of human existence. You came into this world absolutely helpless and were dependent for months and years on the caring love of your parents. Later you tried to develop a sense of independence. You discovered and tested many strategies to assert yourself. But when you see yourself now from higher perspective, you are still just a tiny part bound in the immeasurably vast cosmic course of events. You humbly recognize that your dependence on the whole is a basic aspect of your being.

This card is making you aware of an opportunity to face your experience of existencial helplessness. To do so does not involve

50

any type of sulky resignation. Neither is the game of the misunderstood hero who bravely makes the best of his tough reality expected of you in this situation.

In order to accept your basic helplessness, you need not make yourself small or judge yourself in any way. What is needed here is to pause, to take on the internal and external situation as it is. Only when you are ready to open yourself to what is, whether you like it or not, whether you understand it or not, you will be able to understand and accept yourself and your partner. In this surrender you renounce all desire to change the situation or your relationship. Leave things alone for a while, let the world turn without your assistance and you will see that life develops in wonderful ways without any interference from you. Especially now you can do little except give yourself up to the will of the Whole, and trust.

If you allow your helplessness you can experience a deep sense of security and connection with all of existence.

Question: *In what areas of your relationship are you feeling stagnation or rigidity?*

Suggestion: *Allow yourself and your partner a certain distance from each other for a while. Use the time to let go inside and calmly clarify your situation in the relationship for yourself.*

Affirmation: *I let go and entrust myself and my relationship to the will of the Whole.*

XIII. Death

Key Words: *Parting; intense changes in the relationship; death of the ego; surrender; renewal; rebirth; experience of transcendence.*

The card Death can have several different meanings. The most radical aspect of this card indicates a temporary or final parting from your present partner. If such a parting is in the offing for you, it will come about through external circumstances such as career, education, or travel unless you are aware and decide consciously to separate. If you continue obliviously, some situation will arise to give you both time and space to see how things should proceed. Perhaps your partner will meet someone else and fall in love. In very rare cases this card can also indicate parting through an actual death.

Times of parting are always intense phases in our lives. If you live with a constant awareness of death, you take nothing for granted any longer. The days and hours you spend with your beloved become precious. You see all of eternity in these moments.

The mystics of all times and all schools of thought teach us to bring life into contact with an awareness of death. This enables us to live with an immense intensity and awareness in each present moment. You can arrive at new depth of inner experience. Especially in the presence of death, the fullness of eternal life becomes apparent. Use this time which is a gift, to be together with your partner. Don't try to fight the current. By letting yourself be carried along and remaining awake and conscious, you will find that true surrender does not mean giving yourself up; it is an act of inner power which will take you beyond your former boundaries and limitations.

Death does not mean the end of life. It is a threshold, a passage to new life, to other and greater dimensions of experience; it is the crown and fulfillment of what you have known in your life.

Just as you can experience life in new ways once you feel death's presence, you can discover the dimensions of death by living life totally in the torrential currents of your passionate love. Love and death are actually very close to each other. When you are in a state of deep love, you overcome the fear of death. Only those who have known this experience really know what love is. This is the other aspect of this card. Your love for your partner can become so deep and so strong that in your surrender to that love, something in you dies. You are no longer the person you were before this experience. Your complete surrender to love (love is the only thing to which we can surrender) allows you to experience transcendence. Your ego, i.e., your illusion of being separate from yourself and from the other person, dissolves. The surface which you took to be your identity dies. The Phoenix rises from the ashes.

This experience cannot really be described, because it goes far beyond the world we can grasp and unterstand. Such an ecstatic step is rarely possible at the same moment together with a partner. At first we are alone with our experience, or being left alone catalyses the process. Share this experience only with those people you are sure they will understand you.

The Experience of death can be a passage to a deeper awareness of your existence and to undescribable peak experiences. On the way to that great experience of death may come many smaller deaths. The orgasm, the peak of sexual union, is in some languages called »the little death«. All intense situations and encounters offer us an opportunity to let go, to surrender, to die and be reborn.

Question: *Which of the two major aspects mentioned above (parting or death experience through intense union) is applicable to your relationship?*

Suggestion: *Meditate on this Sufi saying, »Die, before you die!«*

Affirmation: *I am ready to die joyfully in order to be reborn.*

XIV. Art

Key Words: *transformation; change; development; extension; creativity; polar opposites flow together; cosmic love; stillness.*

It can happen during meditation or during a stroll, it can happen when you are alone or while sitting in a group of people. It happens most easily, however, when you are one with a person you love. Then you can experience moments in which you feel accepted, moments in which your desires are fulfilled, moments in which stillness fills you.

The card Art indicates that such moments are possible in your relationship. Your being is transformed just by being close to your beloved. The meeting of your energies sets loose a process of inner alchemy and lets transformation happen. You can extend your perceptions into many areas which most people don't even know exist.

If you find that old patterns are standing in the way of your inner transformation, you have no difficulty in merely stepping over them and continuing on your path. You no longer need to analyze all your possible mistakes and weaknesses. You are able to leave them behind. Your polarity causes no friction. You let the differences flow together and create something new. Your togetherness is like the alchemist's melting pot whose heat dissolves and transforms all disturbing elements. The maturity of your love reveals and develops in your ability to recognize and accept the apparently irreconcilable contradictions in the tensions that exist within each individual, in the relationship between the two of you and between yourselves and the external world.

If you have drawn this card in regard to your current relationship, you can rejoice in the many gifts of this blessed partnership. What good luck that the two of you have found each other! By dealing very consciously with your love, you can help each other on to steps which might have taken years if you had remained alone.

Your relationship is a happening from which something can arise which is bigger than either of you; something which will benefit not only the two of you. The radiance that comes from your inner transformation is received by your environment as well. In a way, your radiance is received by the entire universe.

Question: *How do you recognize what essentially binds you to your partner?*

Suggestion: *Choose with your partner some meditation technique which you can do regularly together.*

Affirmation: *I discover the essence of my relationship and am ready to let the superficial disturbances fall away.*

XV. The Devil

Key Words: *Power and dependency structures; Karmic connections; mutual restrictions; financial dependence; sexual and emotional slavery; misuse of power; duality.*

The Devil is one of the cards whose meanings I unterstood more deeply only after using it in my work to help clarify relationships. For this reason, I would like to add here several important points to supplement my description of the Devil in **Tarot – Mirror of the Soul**.

The Devil is ruled by the Zodiac sign Capricorn, which embodies the principles of extreme crystallization and materialization including all that is solid, earthy, tangible. We can see every day the different temptations with which the Devil tests us – we lose ourselves in material things and forget our connection to the true source and origin of our being. This source is rooted in the more subtle realms. By »seducing« us with material things and bringing into play the duality of good and bad, the Devil actually helps show us the way to find ourselves.

Perhaps an example will make this clear. A fish living in water can become aware of the element surrounding it only if it is taken out and flops around on the land helplessly, feeling death's approach. We live in the cosmic ocean just like a fish in water. When we are thrown out of this ocean and onto the earth, we experience for the first time – often in a very difficult and painful way – that we are separate from that ocean. For the first time, we become aware of the ocean. And when we have wandered around aimlessly long enough, we start looking for the path leading back to our home. Our life on earth – the great experiment in duality – is a cosmic game of becoming aware. The Devil plays a main role in this game.

This by no means is a reason to condemn the material aspect in any way. The path to our essence actually leads through the material. If we don't come to terms with the material world, we cannot grow spiritually. Your inner wealth can only develop if it has an external counterpart. Only when we say an unequivocal »yes« to our earthly existence we can transcend.

When you draw the Devil in regard to a question about a human relationship, it points to power, either obvious or subtle, and dependency structures. Such dark bonds are rarely temporary. Usually unresolved karmic issues have to be brought into the light, and the partners have to liberate themselves from these bonds. Karmic bonds are unresolved entanglements involving blame and guilt. They originated in earlier lives, and in your current relationship they seek purification and resolution.

This card does not predominantly appear in readings about present man-woman relationships. It is usually drawn in relation to unresolved and undissolved ties with important partners who are long gone. This card also plays an important role in pointing out difficult parent-child relationships. Even when one of the partners has died, the undissolved ties can be felt oppressively.

If you draw this card in regard to an ongoing relationship, your most important task is to find out, with your partner, in which areas you experience each other as not free, compulsive, and strained. You both have to realize that you cannot develop your own true potential as long as tremendous amounts of your energies are bound up in the other.

In general, the Devil shows up a conscious or unconscious need to make the partner dependent on you, or a need to be dependent, bound, and not free.

This lack of freedom in couple relationships is usually expressed in one or more of the following three areas:

1. Possessions and material goods
2. Sexuality
3. Striving for influence and power

Material dependence is present when joint property and the general economic standing of the partners is used to bind one partner to the other. A form of bribery takes place when one partner demands certain things of the other. These conflicts can touch on any realm of the partnership; children, household spending, business, or the house. Beneath a cloak of generosity hides a desire to enslave the other. In this same vein, demonstrations of suffering, weakness, and helplessness are all too often a game of blackmail, playing on the gullibility or trustingness and the bad conscience of the partner. If you have drawn the Devil in regard to your present relationship, you need to take a hard and critical look at these areas of your interaction.

Sexual or emotional bondage is so common in man-woman relationships these days that we have come to accept it as normal. Most couples, both married and unmarried, expect the partners to be exclusively there for each other. If one or the other discovers that the partner is also sexually interested in other, the reaction is immediate and violent jealousy. The person's self-worth, even his or her identity can be thrown off balance. No longer centered, he or she strives to win back the »lost« partner either through submission and self-abasement, or through withdrawal of love, distancing, and blackmail.

The mechanisms of emotional and sexual dependence are extremely complex and intricate. The Devil indicates pathological jealousy, sexual power and domination, excessive sexual drive, and lack of trust, openness, and freedom in regard to this problem.

The third area, that of the search for influence and power, is closely tied in to the other two. The emphasis here is on power as a means to gain influence and control over other people. The relationship with a particular partner may serve to further a person's career, for example. The partner is then used as a sign of prestige or an object of show because of his or her strength or social or political (or business) ties.

A relationship with a much weaker partner can, on the other hand, serve to emphasize one's own strength and power. A person in this position tends to surround him or her self with dependent types. This is usually an indication of that person's inability to live out a relationship with anyone on equal terms. Excessive power-seeking can serve to hide a person's own weakness and impotence.

In order to understand all the forms of power and dependence, we have to realize that »perpetrator« and »victim« are two different aspects of the same energy dynamic. The person who plays the role of »victim« searches tirelessly for the »perpetrator« to make him or her whole, until the ideal partner is found. The same is true of the »perpetrator«. If we view this phenomenon in terms of what people radiate and what attracts them, we can see that the energies of the two partners need each other in order to learn through their struggles and eventually to become free through greater awareness. The question of blame or guilt becomes irrelevant.

If you are in any sort of dependence-type relationship which corresponds to the energy of the Devil, your first task is to take responsibility for your own situation. Only when you recognize uncompromisingly your reality you can arrive at a deeper understanding and resolution of the problem.

Question: *In which of the areas mentioned above do you see yourself and your partner entangled?*

Suggestion: *Talk with someone you trust about the situation in your relationship. Find a qualified therapist, if possible together with your partner. The assistance of an experienced expert who has already done work toward his or her own liberation can help you discover the hidden potential for growth contained in your problematic situation. Once all is brought to light, you can make use of what seems now to be a difficult impasse.*

Affirmation: *I recognize my freedom and choose a life in light.*

XVI. The Tower

Key Words: *Destruction of rigid ego and relationship structures; cleansing; purification; change; healing; transformation; renewal; realization, new clarity.*

Dramatic inner changes are imminent in your relationship. They signal their approach with perceivable intensity. It is now impossible to hold on to rigid structures in the same old ways. If you are not ready to drop your habitual expectations, demands, and behaviors, external circumstances will force you to do so. The times in which you were able to impose your demands on your partner or life itself have passed. The issue is no longer to achieve your own wishes and goals at any price! You are being challenged to change your orientation radically. Now is the time to find out in openness and humility which direction existence is directing you – with or without your partner. If you hold on now to egotistical positions or power games, you will create only suffering and pain for yourself and your partner.

The Tower also indicates a great opportunity to give up old, long out-dated structures effortlessly and to let them disappear of their own accord. The time is ripe, and your present situation will help you to recognize which areas of your relationship no

59

longer express your true inner reality. A far-reaching process of transformation is in the offing, and it will affect all realms of your life.

You are now in a phase which necessitates facing an honest and open analysis of your situation. Don't attempt to avoid it. Even if much of what was part of your image must be left behind, what you seem to be losing is only serving the liberation of your true self. Anything in your relationship or your own life which is in harmony with the will of the universe will withstand the storms of life. The issue is one of purification, cleansing and healing of all which expresses your innermost being. The more willingly you enter into this process of change, the sooner you will recognize its deeper meaning. So don't interfere, and trust the wise guidance of your »higher self«.

After a phase of confusion and chaos, you will be able to see your internal and external reality more clearly and understand it. Be grateful to your partner for being there and taking on this important function in your own transformation. By taking full responsibility for your own transformation process, you will also become a vital growth and consciousness-raising influence for your partner. When you draw this card, you and not your partner should be the one to take the first step.

Question: *What areas of your relationship are rigid and stale?*

Suggestion: *Ask your partner to tell you openly and honestly everything he or she has found unsatisfying in your togetherness. Listen without defending yourself, and be open to letting what you hear touch and shake you. Then talk about your own dismay.*

Affirmation: *I let go. I allow.*

XVII. The Star

Key Words: *Cosmic experiences, inspiration; transparency, freedom, space, lightness; visions; shared tasks; radiance.*

If there is someone in your life with whom you can share your love now, let this time of togetherness be one of fulfillment and blessings. Your love should open you both for cosmic experiences.

Whatever touches your heart right now, whether it is a person, a creative activity, an experience of natur or traveling, you will be able to perceive the incident as a divine gift, a sign from God. You feel guided and fulfilled, enriched, and in harmony with cosmic wisdom and intelligence.

The person who is now your partner or the one you will be meeting, can open up new dimensions of life for you. He or she will teach you to see with new eyes. Your companionship will allow you glimpses into realms of being far beyond the boundaries you thought you had until now. You will feel yourself becoming more transparent, more receptive to cosmic inspiration. The experiences now possible with your beloved have a quality of freedom, space, and lightness.

Your shared visions have power and strive to become real. But be careful to take into consideration the laws of the earth. This is necessary in order for your inspirations to crystallize and develop into visible manifestations.

In the case of a partnership which already exists, the Star often indicates a joint or shared task. You need to open yourself to possible ways to share the path toward greater consciousness with other people. The gift of internal growth should never serve to isolate you from other people. Allow those who are also seeking to receive something from you, to whatever extent they are able. Be wary, however, of trying to convince or worse yet, to proselytize others. What you radiate will reach others who are open to and who truly need what you can offer. In this way you simply become open channels for the inspirations of the universe.

The cosmic realms with which you are now in contact are greater than your egos. Give yourself up to them without identifying yourself, or clinging to the experience. Each star sends out its light to the others without doing anything special; each receives the light of others in order to glow in the radiance. You can be stars to light each other's and also other people's paths.

Question: *What comprises the cosmic gifts given you in your relationship?*

Suggestion: *Allow yourselves regular times for silence, reflection and meditation. Go to events, or places, or situations which inspire you.*

Affirmation: *Together we realize our cosmic inspirations.*

XVIII. The Moon

Key Words: *Confronting the shadowy side; hard tests; possibility to be liberated from karmic entanglements; transformation; from the darkness into the light.*

Unconsciously you may have felt it all along. There is something about your partner which attracts you very much and at the same time scares you. You should concern yourselves now a little more with this »something«.

Your relationship is in a critical phase, a time of hard tests. You and your partner now have to confront the shadowy sides of yourselves which you probably have repressed or denied for a long time. Karmic difficulties may become manifested in current happenings. You should stop avoiding dealing with this.

You already know most of your important partners from earlier lives. In these situations, your relationships quickly develop a certain depth. You are also, however, karmically »burdened« from the start, and an important aspect of your relationship consists of making good old karmic debts. If your partner hurts you, you may feel the same pain which you caused him or her in an earlier life. This game of revenge and mutual injury does not, however, have to go on endlessly.

To burn off unresolved karma you need a great deal of personal power and clarity. We arrive at these trough meditation and directed therapeutic work. This card is showing you that you and your partner have a chance to make a deciding leap into greater realization and consciousness. If you are really ready to get to know your shadowy aspects, and walk through them together, your efforts will be well rewarded. Your relationship will undergo a deep and far reaching transformation process. By freeing yourselves of karma, you come a great deal closer to your own fulfillment. We are living in a time when we can throw off the ballast of centuries, in order to be free to take a great step into a new age.

The Moon represents a last hurdle which must be jumped. In his story »Vor dem Gesetz« Franz Kafka tells of a man who waits his whole life to be let through an open gate by the gate guard. The man sits for days and years. He begs and curses, he threatens and complains, but he is denied entrance to the law (German: Gesetz = law). Only when he is at death's door, does the guard lean over to him to growl, »This entrance was only for you. Now i will go and lock it«. This card is calling you: Don't listen to your gate guard, pass through the narrow opening, go through the guarded gate into the unknown!

Question: *What are the shadowy aspects of your relationship?*

Suggestion: *Meditate regularly, when possible, with your partner. Note the quality of the images and thoughts you have, and discuss them. Take note also of your dreams. Possibly find a therapist to support your work.*

Affirmation: *By walking through the darkness, I arrive at the light.*

XIX. The Sun

Key Words: *Highly creative energy; liberation; transformation; openess; innocence; joy in living; ecstasy; realization; wisdom; spirituality; mature love.*

The Sun is the highest energy card in the Tarot, and for a relationship, it depicts one of the strongest and most beautiful images. Now is the time for joy and celebration! You can rejoice with your partner and enjoy his or her presence totally.

The two naked dancing children on the mountain of creativity depict a partnership which is liberated from all and any constraints and compulsions. This liberation expresses itself through ecstatic joy and enthusiasm. All energies are now free to be used wholeheartedly and unrestrictedly in the service of your joint creativity. These energies are no longer wasted in struggles for domination, in jealousy or in withdrawal, and creating boundaries.

In your relationship, a liberating opening is possible. A far reaching alchemical transformation process is in the works. If you are both receptive to it, the sun can come up in your relationship and can shine with a strong clear light.

The sun represents the highest degree of consciousness, wisdom, enlightenment, and divine love. As the central point of our planetary system, it possesses powerful centering qualities. It is the highest representative of the element fire and embodies its qualities of warmth, light, creativity, purification, and transformation.

All doors to a fulfilled love relationship are now opened to you and your partner. The most important characteristics of a relationship permeated with the Sun's energy are creativity and joy in living! Any difficulties or conflicts you may have can now be seen in the proper light, so they can loose their heavy and bitter seriousness. Your love becomes light, playful, and humorous, and gives each of you a tremendous sense of freedom.

The Sun's light is a transforming force which easily dissolves old limiting structures, like the warmth of spring which liberates the land from snow and ice after every winter. The Sun's light removes the frozen and rigid structures of a relationship and allows the waters of emotion to flow freely again.

So be ready now to leave behind the long outgrown structures in your relationship. Begin again from the first step, and learn something from the wisdom and innocence of children. You can enjoy the celebration of your ecstatic liberation together only if you are both ready to undergo this deep and farreaching transformation process at the same time. If one of the partners clings stubbornly and desperately to old, unconscious patterns, the Sun's energy can easily end the relationship if that is what the other partner needs in order to follow his or her freedom. This force can bring everything which is false, untrue, and unreal into the light so that both people have to face reality and come to a decision.

The Sun is the energy of love that brings into the light anything incompatible with this energy. Only a pure heart, with the open and vulnerable innocence of a child, can stand its ground in front of this all-pervading reality.

Question: *Are there still dark areas in your relationship? In which of them are you now ready to bring light?*

Suggestion: *Take the time to share your thoughts and feelings lovingly and openly with your partner about your relationship. Tell each other which areas in your togetherness feel unfree, and be especially careful to hear each other out patiently while speaking about yourselves and your feelings. If you are really open with each other, you will find that airing even the painful* *and scary aspects of your thoughts can be liberating. Bring light into the dark corners of your relationship and then find out how you would like to celebrate your togetherness.*

Affirmation: *In my openness and vulnerability lies the power which renews and rejuvenates everything.*

XX. The Aeon

Key Words: *Letting judgements fall; acceptance through increased perception; recognition of the larger inter-relationships; surrender to cosmic love; empathy; wisdom; honesty; trust in the divine plan.*

Your relationship is full of mystery, just as this card is. You can view this as awed children or as wise initiates. Enter more and more deeply into this mystery!

Whoever draws this card is in a phase in which it is possible to fathom the mysteries of his or her relationship. All events, both past and present, can be viewed from a higher perspective now. Your intimations for the future become certainties. You can perceive your relationship in a new light, and you can also develop an understanding of the powers which have brought you together with your partner.

Perhaps you are faced with many puzzles. If you remain silent and simply perceive, the mirror of your expanding awareness will open up new dimensions of inner realization and wisdom. The calm of certainty pervades your being. Trusting in the greater purpose of all changing manifestations, you develop the ability to surrender to yourself and the reality of your relationship. There is nothing special to do. Just accept the grace of this moment thankfully, and honor and shelter it.

Your broadened perception shows you an opportunity to let go of values and judgments. There is nothing to change or criticize in your partner. In recognizing profoundly that everything is just as it should be, you accept unconditionally your self, your partner, and the reality of your relation.

When judgement ends, perception becomes that much clearer and deeper. This card does not suggest that you simply ignore your partner's failings and weaknesses. On the contrary, when you understand and accept the other completely, you become much more able to express your own feelings and perceptions without any inappropriate considerations or constraints based on a need to be »polite«. You can communicate in ways that allow your partner to feel your deep acceptance of him or her, and make your words an aid toward greater awareness and learning.

There are two important »side-effects« connected with this state of recognition. In this state, you always feel very calm and clear, never angry, sad, or fearful. You also are always able to see how the things you are perceiving elsewhere correspond to you and your own situation. When we look at far horizons, we are also looking deeply into ourselves.

Letting go of judgements and expanding your own perceptions are two milestones on the way to the center of this card – harmony with cosmic love. The goal of your relationship is no less than that. You both have probably had a taste of this love, either through shared experiences in earlier lives or through especially deep moments in your present relationship. Instead of slipping from being in love into just being used to each other, you now have a chance to join in the cosmic dance and experience oneness with all that is.

Question: *What is the leitmotif, the central theme of your relationship?*

Suggestion: *Talk with your partner about how your relationship came about and how it has developed until now. Together, find the threads, the themes which run through it all and give that special quality to your relationship. Examine also which mee-*

tings you have had in earlier lives are of importance in your present relationship.

Affirmation: *Everything is as it should be.*

XXI. The Universe

Key Words: *Cosmic love; liberation; boundlessness; openess; All-One, union; completion; transformation; a new beginning; naturalness; independence; deep trust.*

What more can you want of a relationship? Whether you know it or not, right now you are finding in your partner all which the universe holds for you. How much of this immeasurable gift you take on depends entirely on you. The world is open for you and invites you to dance in the cosmic round.

The sort of liberation you are experiencing together reaches far beyond any ideas you had about freedom. You and your partner are in a position to let go of old fears. Fear creates tension, tightness inside you. Every time you let go of a fear, you create an inner space, an openness, a »yes« to whatever comes. This »yes«» is so universal that it includes and transcends existing structures (Saturn).

Nothing in your environment, your relationship or your partner, needs to change. If you look intuitively you will see that everything is exactly as it should be. This recognition can spread like an explosion within you. Your willingness to love carries you beyond the limitations of the past.

A great learning cycle in your relationship is drawing to its conclusion. The completion is also a new beginning on a higher plane of being. You are coming one step closer to the ultimate goal – the return to the source of cosmis oneness.

You are now able to realize how unnecessary it is for you to disguise, to »dress up« or to mask yourself. Instead, you are open and fully surrendered; in this way you get to know new realms both in yourself and in your loved one. You are bound together with your original purity, and can let yourself be caught up in the whirling dance of the ever-moving universe. The boundaries of the small »I« become permeable. Orgasmic union with your partner becomes a cosmic experience.

Whatever you wish to realize now with your partner will be blessed with success on all levels as long as it is in accordance with the will of the universe.

Question: *How does your liberation express itself in your relationship with your partner?*

Suggestion: *If you wish to achieve something special with your partner, begin now to put your plans in concrete forms and realize your goals.*

Affirmation: *I am now open for great fulfillment.*

B. The Court Cards

Knight of Wands

Key Words: *Dynamic fire; cleansing, purification; aggressive potential as creative expression.*

Whatever is on the agenda in your relationship, give your entire power and dynamic energy to it! What you are trying to achive demands your total commitment. You have all the power you need to take the next important step.

Negativity and obstructive fears have to be swept out of your way. These may involve your inner fears as well as those related to the dynamics of your relationship.

When you draw this card, you are deeply motivated and prepared to overcome all existing difficulties. The cleansing power of fire will help you to recognize and purify all such areas. They are the obstacles and barriers preventing your relationship from developing on the way to true and satisfying togetherness.

If you are a man drawing this card, the issue is to set free your male fire. Give total expression to your energies, whether through your sexuality or through some creative act. The woman who really love you will value the liberation of your energies.

If you are a woman drawing this card, it may be showing that you seek the above-mentioned qualities in a man. Don't forget that the external qualities which attract you or which you feel are lacking around you are reflections of inner qualities which you have to develop in yourself as well. As you become familiar with your inner man, you also support your external partner to develop his own male qualities.

Question: *In what areas of your relationship do you tend to be »considerated« of your partner in an inappropriate way? What fears are at the root of this behavior?*

Suggestion: *Invent playful ways for you to show each other your aggression. Afterwards, talk about in which areas you tend to hold back your energies.*

Affirmation: *I express and live out my power and dynamism freely and openly.*

Queen of Wands

Key Words: *Sympathy; dignity; loving presence; self-knowledge; love matured by tests; ability to be there for another person.*

The times are passed in which your relationships were marked by neediness and dependency. You have been trough many experiences, some painful, which have led you to deeper levels of yourself. You know that your ultimate fulfillment is to be found, not in others, but only in yourself. This gives you an easiness, a certain presence, from which you can easily share with other people.

You come to your partner with a sense of fullness and power arising from the love which has been so harshly tested. You no longer feel inwardly deficient.

Your internal fulfillment is no longer called into question by the mistakes and weaknesses of your partner. The remembrance of your own tests has given you deep compassion, so you can accept your partner lovingly, with all his or her weaknesses. In your partner's times of crisis you can be a loving and supportive companion.

This card my be drawn while you are in the midst of a crisis in your relationship. In this case, it is an indication that the painful experiences you are going through are part of a transformatory learning process. Accept them with dignity and gratitude. This is a time of testing. The fruits of tests will be seen only after you have passed through this phase.

Question: *What insights and qualities have been matured in you during times of trials and testing?*

Suggestion: *Remember times in your relationship during which your love was tested by painful experiences.*

Affirmation: *I pass on to others what life has taught me.*

Prince of Wands

Key Words: *Trust; openness; freedom; lightness; joy of life; fiery sensuality; seeing with the heart.*

Openness, trust and blossoming love are the qualities of the heart which the Prince of Wands brings to expression as no other card does. The partner is seen through the eyes of the heart which do not judge or condemn. There is space for you to feel oneness and joy in living.

The potential for growth and experience on your shared path seems endless now. The whole world is open to you. Optimism and lightness fill all realms of your being. Now you can take on tasks with your partner which you would not dare to usually.

The realm of sensuality also takes on a playful lightness. You express your desires and needs openly and freely. Any problems between you and your beloved fade into the background. You have a chance to allow your love to blossom free of cares and fears.

Question: *How do your perceptions change when you see the people close to you with the eyes of your heart?*

Suggestion: *Sit opposite each other in an open position. Let your breath flow deeply and gently into your heart center. Open* *your arms and hands to each other and let your bodies follow their impulses. Let everything happen between you in a mood of playful lightness. In order to get beyond the usual manipulation impulse, repeat the exercise three times, returning to the beginning position each time. Give yourselves time! You will find that with each new attempt, your impulses become more authentic, and will bring you closer to the deeper levels.*

Affirmation: *I see with the eyes of my heart.*

Princess of Wands

Key Words: *Freedom for fear; capacity for ecstasy; new beginning; joy of life; passionateness; openness.*

You have been the victim of your fear far too long. Fear and love can not exist at the same time. Fear leaves no room for love. But now the flames of your love are being fanned anew, and your fears disappear.

The Princess of Wands represents youthful, tempestuous love. You are now in a position to leave fears behind and give yourself up to your burning passion. You may focus on a new partner or on life itself.

You feel open toward all people who are close to you, and toward those you meet now. You play fearlessly with all possibilities. Conventional, safe patterns of behavior are irrelevant for you now. When you surrender ecstatically to love, you no longer look for the secure or safe path. You trust your own feelings and are protected by that which you radiate and give to ohters.

If you are in a relationship now, you can show yourself openly and fearlessly to your partner. Your openness will also help your partner show you aspects of himself or herself which have remained hidden until now.

75

Liberation from fear always creates a new beginning. Unsatisfying relationships can be ended fearlessly. You know that you really are losing nothing. Instead, you are opening yourself for new contacts which correspond to your deeper needs.

Question: *What fears have prevented you in the past from developing your capacity for love?*

Suggestion: *Spend more time than usual with other people. Show yourself fearlessly, and play with all your possibilities.*

Affirmation: *As I surrender to my love, my fears disappear.*

Knight of Cups

Key Words: *Family; family of your choosing; life partnerships; spiritual community; opening and expanding the relationship.*

Your relationship is in the process of opening and expanding. The themes of »family« and »choosing your own family« take on meaning and importance.

This card can indicate that the time has come for you and your partner to think about starting a family. If you already live in a family situation, the card is urging you to give more of your time and energy to family affairs. You can find deep fulfillment in this part of your life now.

This card also often points to a »family of choice«. This can be a community of people or a group of people who have similar goals and views. With them you find interchange, stimulation, deep friedship and help for your spiritual growth. Connecting with such a group of people will be a tremendous enrichment of your relationship. You will be able to grow beyond the bounds of your twosomeness and find new activities and new perspectives for your shared path.

If your partner is not ready now to join in with such a group, don't let yourself be held back from fulfilling your own needs to meet with other travelers on the path. The gifts which may be awaiting you will make your leap into new planes of emotional exchange very worthwhile.

Question: *What are your desires, ideas and ideals in relation to a family or community living situation?*

Suggestion: *Examine whether this card relates to your own family or to a »chosen« family. Talk with your partner about your views and desires.*

Affirmation: *I am open for a community which will fulfill and enrich me.*

Queen of Cups

Key Words: *Great empathy; subtle, fine perception; motherliness; a giving love; emotional independence.*

The aspects of motherliness and deep empathy become very important in your relationship now. Superficiality is not satisfying at the moment. The desire to melt together is growing. You have a deep-rooted need to leave the planes of analytical thinking in order to experience the deeper mysteries of your relationship.

If you want to delve into the secrets of your intimate connections to another person, you have to enter deeply into the realm of feelings and sensitivity. Blossoming love expresses itself in many different froms. The Queen of Cups represents a subtle, fine togetherness based on real emotional surrender.

If your readiness finds resonance in your partner, you can now meet on much deeper levels. Your yearning for this deeper meeting may also, however, meet with resistance and distance on your partner's part. This often happens when a person has not resolved some aspects of his or her relationship with the mother. Your partner may be afraid of being stifled and monopolized. This is the fear of losing one's own identity when dissolving the boundaries of the self, and no longer being able to make delineations between the self and the rest of existence.

In any case, it is now very important to talk openly about your needs or fears with each other, without setting the other under pressure in any way.

The Queen of Cups bears a tremendous potential for giving love. She brings this inner quality out, without concern for other people's fears or weaknesses. If you draw this card, take it as an indication that you also carry this strength within you, and should develop it further.

Question: *How do you show your soft and sensitive side in your relationship?*

Suggestion: *With your partner, think about ways you could lavish attention on each other. Be sure that you provide an opportunity for each to be the giver and the receiver.*

Affirmation: *Light and love permeate my being.*

Prince of Cups

Key Words: *Animal sexuality; passion, desire, craving, dominated by physical urges; possibility of transformation.*

This card confronts you with your sexuality and passion. The lesson to be learned now is a meaningful one, and bears within it a possibility of transformation.

Sexual energy is a fundamental energy. It is part of the creation of all life on this planet and is a close part of us from the moment we are born. Every cell of our bodies is permeated with this energy.

Paradoxically, our culture is tremendously preoccupied with fighting this primal energy, or repressing it. This struggle is, however, useless and destructive because it is directed against life itself.

Sex calls awake your animal powers; your wildness, your lust, your greed, your physical urges, your desire to embody another being. This may frighten you. When you draw this card, it is a clear invitation to stop avoiding these realms. Instead of judging and fighting them, you can transform your sexual energy by accepting it and giving it open expression.

Be aware of your desires! This will give you the chance to grow beyond yourself.

If you have a partner who also enjoys sharing with you all the realms of sexuality and passion, use this opportunity to experiment playfully with these energies.

Sexual union expresses a primal desire for oneness, for an end to our separation. By tasting your physical union with all your senses, you can get a taste of transcendence, of being one with all of existence. This experience alters you and transforms sexual energy more and more into universal love.

If you cannot express your sexual needs with anyone now, you may be in danger of directing your sexual energy destructively and punitively against yourself or others. You can escape this danger by simply standing by yourself now.

If you cannot express your sexual desires with a partner, be open for other, creative and meditative expressions of that energy. Life is offering you a great opportunity to experience other forms of energy transformation. Just be sure you aren't using your creativity and meditation to escape or to deny your sexual impulses.

Question: *What are your strongest sexual desires and fantasies?*

Suggestion: *Talk with your partner about your »secret« sexual desires and fantasies. Have the courage to be honest and risk something!*

Affirmation: *In conscious acceptance of my sexuality, I experience transformation and unity.*

Princess of Cups

Key Words: *Overcoming jealousy and possessiveness; self trust, self confidence; blossoming love; harmony.*

The feelings which in the past limited your openess and freedom have been overcome, or you are in the process of letting them go. You have gotten to know jealousy, possessiveness, control, and power games and are now ready to let go of those chains with which you sought to bind your partner to you. In this gentle liberation, your real love can blossom.

You see past and present difficulties with new, clear eyes, and you are increasingly willing to do without fighting and manipulations. By recognizing your own value, you gain self confidence. You feel free and are ready to allow your beloved some free room. This will allow you, in turn, to accept your partner as he or she is.

Harmony and love fill your being. You are in harmony with

yourself and your surroundings. Your relationship gains independence and trusting openness because of these inner qualities.

Question: *What supports you in the process of accepting yourself?*

Suggestion: *Sit opposite your partner and meditate. Feel your own worth and inner beauty. Allow your body to express this through harmonious movements. Show yourself in all your beauty to your partner.*

Affirmation: *I allow myself and my beloved freedom.*

Knight of Swords

Key Words: *Goal orientation; high ideals; reminder to be patient and check things out; danger of impatience.*

You have clear, set ideas which you would like to reach and realize with your partner. This may be a goal in terms of your relationship's form, or a project you would like to enter together, or a task or direction in life you both share. You pursue these ideas, fantasies or expectations doggedly, without looking to the left or right.

If your partner shares your definite commitment and your ideals are identical, you will realize your goals very quickly. If your goals are not identical, however, tremendous tension may result. Your partner may feel overwhelmed or overpowered by your impatience and may react with resistance or even withdrawal.

Instead of taking time to carefully examine the »Lay of the land« you are much more inclined to push through your set ideas and goals with dogged determination. But those ideas and goals which express your true inner reality cannot be realized in this manner. Your blinders prevent you perceiving what your partner's inner and outer reality are.

When you draw this card, be sure to measure your own ideals against concrete realities. Recognize and take into consideration all aspects of your particular situation. If you do so, you will find your original goals changing somewhat. Your horizons will broaden along with your awareness. Whatever you will be able to do with your partner will become a gift that is not to be taken for granted.

The aspects of your ideals and desires that can not be fulfilled at this time in your relationship must not necessarily be set aside as being unrealistic. Let them keep working inside you, taking hold with time. If they are clear and realistic, they will bear fruit at the appropriate time.

Question: *Are you and your partner in agreement about your goals?*

Suggestion: *Take some time to discuss your present wishes and goals.*

Affirmation: *I achieve my goals in harmony with my partner.*

Queen of Swords

Key Words: *Liberation from masks and roles; honesty; openness; courage; clarity.*

In your relationship, you are striving for greater clarity. You are prepared to destroy or drop old masks in order to achieve this new clarity. Until now, you and your partner have been more or less successful at hiding behind certain masks.

The same is true of the role-playing which goes on in almost every relationship because of childhood conditioning or unconscious fears. These unspoken and unwritten »contracts« function by lending apparent stability to a relationship. But they can all too easily become confining, a sort of prison which prevents your growth. This becomes obvious the moment you and your partner decide that your development as individuals is more important than clinging to your shared sense of security.

When you begin to glimpse your true faces, you may initially be shocked by what you see. Perhaps you have lived for a long time with certain convenient lies or dishonesties. The time has come to speak the truth and show yourselves as you are. Caution and falsness will be your greatest obstacles in this phase of your journey toward honesty, openness and authenticity.

If you avoid unnecessary caution and all forms of »hide-and-seek«, you will reach new depths and new clarity in your relationship. Now you need the kind of courage and love which know that what is part of your deepest truth can never be destroyed. Perhaps much of what belongs to the more superficial planes will be left by the wayside, and these losses may seem very painful to you and/or your partner. Just remember that letting go of the superficial will serve to bring you closer to your true reality. The more honest you are with yourself and your partner now, the greater your chances of attaining a true meeting on deeper planes.

yourself be restricted, or getting involved or committed to things which you haven't chosen out of your own deeper convictions. If you maintain an appropriate balance between structure and freedom, even the most strenuous of undertakings will become a worthwhile gift of personal growth.

If there are no difficult tasks or crisis in your relationship now, this card can be seen as an invitation to explore what projects the two of you could take up together.

Question: *Are there duties or responsibilities in your relationship which you find restricting?*

Suggestion: *Talk with your partner about which of these responsibilities must be met and which problems must be solved.*

Affirmation: *The effort I expend on this relationship serves to further our shared growth.*

Queen of Disks

Key Words: *Recuperation; relaxation; rest; enjoyment; physicality, fruitfulness; vacation; mental and physical regeneration.*

In this relationship, or in earlier ones, you have had a lot of trouble. Behind you lies a long and weary path through the desert of heavy emotions. Now a moment has arrived in which you and your partner can rest and take a breath. There is nothing in particular to do or accomplish, but a great deal to enjoy.

The Queen of Disks emphasizes the aspects of physical regeneration and renewal. You should arrange things with your partner so that you can spend time giving and receiving the emotional and physical nourishment you need so much.

If this is not possible within your present relationship, this card encourages you to take a vacation from your partner. Find a restful and rejuvenating place in which you can just switch yourself off and gain some peace and distance form the tensions you cannot escape in your daily life. You can also receive support by being around people you can enjoy in a relaxed and easy fashion.

If you feel well and comfortable with your partner, your relationship is a place of fruitfulness for you.

The children you bring into the world together must not necessarily be made of flesh and blood. You may conceive »children« on a spiritual or mental level. But these children will thrive only if their parents are doing well. The parents will do well if they are loving and attentive to themselves – you can give to others only what you have learned to give to yourself.

Question: *How can you rest and rejuvenate yourself best now? Will it include your partner?*

Suggestion: *Take a lot of time to decide with your partner how you can best pamper each other. If you cannot do this with your partner now, take time for your own vacation and relaxation.*

Affirmation: *I let go and relax. There is nothing to do, but much to enjoy.*

Prince of Disks

Key Words: *Physicality; earthy power; body-oriented sensuality; danger of identification with the material plane.*

The aspects brought into focus by this card are centered around the body and material interests. These can be thoroughly beautiful, yet they also carry a certain amount of danger. You have to decide for yourself in which direction this card is addressing you.

The positive potential of these physical aspects includes your ability to enjoy the body and your physical nature with your partner. Together you can explore and develop this part of your being. You just feel physically well when you are together. You enjoy food and sex with him or her in a way you can with no one else. You feel nourished, protected, and in good hands. Your body is refreshed, reenergized, and healed. You also support each other financially and give generous gifts.

The danger of such a situation lie in the tendency to overemphasize the material plane. You may start to identify yourselves with the physical exclusively, and end up going in circles. Sooner or later you will feel overfull, sated, and bored. If you direct your ambitions only toward the satisfaction of physical, sensual desires and the acquisition of material possessions, these realms cease to be a source of fulfillment and become burdensome and confining. The senses are meant to be stimulated and enlivened, but when overstimulated they make you feel heavy and dulled. In time you will have to recognize that confining your attention to the material plane causes many other levels of your being to atrophy.

This card is an invitation to bring the realms related to the earth into closer contact with meditation (compare with the Ace of Disks). The material should serve as a basis for our spiritual growth. You can see your physical wellbeing as a prerequisite for meditation and growth of consciousness. The love you express toward your body by taking good care of it is an appropriate expression of appreciation for the physical aspect of your nature. In this way, the earth becomes a bearer of spirit, and the body becomes the temple of the soul.

Question: *What value do you give to the physical and material plane in your relationship?*

Suggestion: *Look critically at whether the physical and material aspects of your relationship encourage or hinder your self-development.*

Affirmation: *My body is my temple.*

Princess of Disks

Key Words: *Harmony; renewal; pregnancy; preparation; inspiration; the relationship as a source of strength and power; harmonious interchange.*

Slowly, almost imperceptibly, something is changing in your relationship. Then, suddenly, there will be a breakthrough to a new kind of togetherness. You are in a phase where the new is slowly growing, but has not yet taken on any concrete visible form. This is a time of preparation, and, if you will, »pregnancy«.

In your togetherness, your inner harmony is growing and becoming a source of inspiration and perception. You experience aspects of yourself in your relationship which otherwise hardly ever come to light. The presence of your partner encourages you to find yourself and helps you realize your ideas.

Your masculine and feminine energies are harmoniously balanced and together bring about the renewal and development of important parts of your being.

You can make your relationship something »holy« by letting

it be a place of power which helps you realize your connection to the universe. In order for this to be possible, you have to spend time to become really open and familiar with each other.

You may feel the need to be with your partner now more than usual. Give in to that need, even if it means letting other interests rest for the time being. What you are gaining in your exchange of energies is very valuable and enriching.

Question: *What is the basis of the support you are given by your partner?*

Suggestion: *Tell your partner what new aspects of yourself are being developed through your relationship and his or her support.*

Affirmation: *I find my power, strength, and harmony in my relationship with my beloved. My love is the source of my power.*

C. The Minor Arcana

Wands
Cups
Swords
Disks

Ace of Wands

Key Words: *Energy; fiery relationship; great potential; sexual vitality; possibility of transformation; drive toward action, initiative; passion.*

The card shows a strudy wand, surrounded by lightning bolts, with tongues of flame blazing from it. What could this mean for you and your partner?

Tremendous energy is flowing between you and the person who attracts you. This is the energy of fire, both destructive and, at the same time, creative.

Your interaction is characterized by great intensity. Depending on the present phase of your relationship, certain areas within you and your partner will »catch fire« now. You may become enflamed with passion and enthusiasm for each other or for some shared issue. But if fundamental areas are blocked or disturbed, they will instead become enflamed and explosive. The flames of the conflicts that will then arise between you will burn out whatever is untrue and impure. Such conflicts bear great creative potential. They serve the purpose of cleansing and liberation.

You now have the chance to bring light into your shadowy side and to transform important aspects of yourselves. This is particularly true of your sexuality. Don't just waste your sexual energy. Become more and more conscious in your expression of it. Tantra may play an important part in your development of greater awareness in sex.

Basically, you and your partner should be clear about which goal you »burn« for, and in which internal and external directions you wish to aim your energies.

Question: *What inner realms does your partner set on fire in you?*

Suggestion: *Do an active meditation with your partner for a period of time. The best is the »Dynamic Meditation«.*

Affirmation: *I share my fiery power with my partner.*

Two of Wands – Dominion

Key Words: *Warrior energy; faultless fight; centeredness; self-control; energetic undertakings.*

Mars in his own sign, Aries, testifies to the presence of a war-like, energetic force which is unconditionally and unimpeachably directed toward achieving the goals at hand.

In terms of a relationship, this can indicate constructive and creative debate and discussion with your partner. Sparks may fly in the heat of the fencing match, but don't lose your self-control for even an instant. Express your point of view, stand up for your rights, but never allow the argument to throw you off balance, to make you lose your center, your dignity, and your clarity.

The circumstances which have sparked this conflict are, if you look closely, not as meaningful as you think they are. More important than a victory is the manner in which you fight. Every honest confrontation staged openly brings you closer to your partner and gives depth to your relationship. Be sure, then, in the midst of the struggle not to close your heart. Conduct the exchange of arguments as an energetic exchange of blows. In this way you can enjoy even an argument with your partner. Part of getting to know each other is measuring each other's power in battle!

If you have no particular conflicts at the moment, use this energy now available to you in some joint, active undertaking.

Question: *Have you ever had the experience of enjoying a fight or argument with your partner?*

Suggestion: *When you have your next argument, try consciously to make it a creative act.*

Affirmation: *Even in a fight, my heart remains open.*

Three of Wands – Virtue

Key Words: *Centeredness; purity; faultlessness; new beginning; trust; vitality; realness; harmony.*

You can start anew with your partner. The Three of Wands shows that the air between you is clear now. You have enough self-confidence and power to be centered and relaxed with your partner. You also know that you don't need to prove yourself or push yourself into the forefront.

Your feeling for what is real is well developed, and you can find the point where tolerance ends and lazy compromise begins, by remaining in tune with your own center. Aligned with your inner strenght, you no longer can be satisfied with half-heartedness. The more you trust yourself, the more deeply you will be able to trust in your relationship.

Inner peace and equanimity combine harmoniously with joy of life and vitality. You radiate cheerfulness which will probably soon ruf off on your partner. Your partner feels well in your presence, and you can share your harmony with other people as well.

Question: *In what way would you like to begin anew with your partner?*

Suggestion: *Take a restful evening for yourselves, spread a blanket on the floor, and give each other intuitive massages.*

Affirmation: *I am at peace within, and I am open.*

Four of Wands – Completion

Key Words: *Conclusion; new beginning on higher planes; creativity; integration of opposites; unification, completion.*

You now have the opportunity in your relationship to complete a cycle and ready yourself for new adventures. In order to really complete old business and make it a springboard for your new adventures, you have to be sure that all open issues in your relationship are clarified now. Do this in a fashion both direct and loving.

Your partner helps you in your personal journey toward completion by representing the opposite pole for you. The sense of fulfillment you can experience with this other person is a mirror of the potential within you for wholeness. You have sought and found this partner to help you develop the opposing aspects of yourself. Your present situation serves primarily to facilitate this process.

Rather than wasting your energies with silly little arguements about trifles, learn to accept your partner's differentness without wanting to change him or her. There is a tremendous amount of creative force in your relationship which can develop and grow much more easily if you allow your opposite sides to flow together. If there is tension, now is a good time to purify and de-fuse it. You can be open for new impulses, for a new beginning on higher planes.

Question: *Are you prepared and willing to accept your partner's differentness? What areas are in urgent need of clarification or completion?*

Suggestion: *Share openly with your partner in which areas you find him or her opposite to you, and in what ways this polarity helps make you whole.*

Affirmation: *By accepting polar opposites I become complete.*

Five of Wands – Strife

Key Words: *Inhibited strife; tension; conflict; vain effort; struggle and fight, or resignation; blocked energy; chance to be reminded of your own power.*

When you draw the Five of Wands in regard to an existing relationship, it points to a massive internal conflict concerning your partner. Maybe you are full of ideas, plans and demands and would like to realize them in your relationship at any price. You strive to move forward, and try to win your partner over to your way of doing things. You want to set your partner in motion toward your goals and interests. You are assuming that the fulfillment you seek is only possible if your partner supports you completely and wholeheartedly.

But instead of sharing your enthusiasm, your partner becomes reserved and withdrawn. You experience him or her as a sort of emergency brake, constantly opposing your tremendous impulses at the decisive moment. His or her behavior seems, either overtly or covertly, authoritarian. This reminds you of your childhood, when your parents or other authority figures suffocated your joy in life and your drive toward freedom with their restrictions.

The more you struggle against your partner's limiting behavior, the more your partner will close off to you. You can't force your will on your partner without severely damaging the relationship. There may be extreme situations in which the destruction of old structures is the only way out of your prison, but usually there are other, more constructive ways.

Instead of fighting your partner or resigning and giving up, take time and space to seek out your own internal space. There you can discover much more power than you might have thought you possessed. When you are in touch with your true strength, you are free, independent, and capable of realizing everything which is worth striving for in your life. When your partner no longer feels under pressure, you will have less difficulty drawing him or her in and winning him or her over to your ideas.

You may also be experiencing this conflict in the opposite circumstances, with you being the one trying to put the brakes on your partner's forward impulses. In this case, be sure to observe you fears as they arise because of your partner's behavior and desires.

Question: *How does the conflict between striving and restraining manifest in your relationship?*

Suggestion: *Examine in which areas and situations you feel repressed or pressured by your partner. Write down what you recognize and take quiet time to talk these patterns over.*

Affirmation: *Trusting in my inner strength, I go my way.*

Six of Wands – Victory

Key Words: *Victory; breakthrough; success; energies set free; strength through togetherness; confidence.*

Your relationship may sometimes seem to be a lot of trouble, but your efforts are worthwhile. After phases of conflict and struggle there are sudden unexpected moments when everything becomes very easy, playful, and pleasurable. Such a moment is possible for you now. What you have worked for in your relationship can become a reality now. You have spent a lot of time and energy toward making things work; now you can experience the sudden breakthrough. Victory comes out of the blue.

You can feel the energies each of you has set free in the other. Enjoy and savor your togetherness as intensively as possible. You can also gain an inkling of what further, and greater victories are possible for you.

A fire is burning within you both – one which blazes without your having to fan the flames through confrontations or other artificial means. You need only to free the fire from burned-out ashes and let it become one with your partner's flames. This means to share everything that is important to you, and find ways of living your strength together.

Question: *What does »victory« mean to you in relation to your partner?*

Suggestion: *Share with your partner your ideas about how your victory will look.*

Affirmation: *My victory is also my partner's victory.*

Seven of Wands – Valour

Key Words: *Strength; energy; courage; uncompromising; mutual strengthening; power; achievement, carrying through; self confidence; flawlessness; honesty.*

Mars in Leo indicates a warlike energy which manifests itself through a tremendous force for carrying through and accomplishing. Whatever is happening in your relationship you now have sufficient courage and willingness to risk something in order to represent successfully your own inner reality and to achieve your goals. When you can stand up openly and unimpeachably for your own intentions, you enable your partner to do the same. You can discuss and debate in a fair way. The point is no longer who wins or loses; the intensity and honesty of your encounter gives you both the opportunity to find out from each other what you really want.

You can now take a risk in your relationship by telling your partner clearly, without beating around the bush, exactly what you want. If you stand by yourself, nothing and no one can shake you. Have faith in yourself, trust yourself to represent your interests definitely and uncompromisingly.

Each of you needs to allow and develop your own inner power. The more you do so individually, the stronger you become together. If you have a shared goal connecting you, your combined powers can help you now to accomplish what you want to, without being misled or distracted by outsiders.

Question: *Do you live out your inner reality in your relationship?*

Suggestion: *With your partner, go to a self-help group which is oriented toward »encounter«. If this is not possible, take 30 minutes in which to sit opposite each other and tell each other openly and honestly what you want. When one is speaking, the other should just listen without interrupting or reacting.*

Affirmation: *I stand by myself openly and honestly, which gives my partner the opportunity to do the same for himself (herself).*

Eight of Wands – Swiftness

Key Words: *Movement; directness; decisiveness; possibility for clarification; open communication; flexibility.*

At the moment you are involved in a turbulent relationship in which the situation can change very quickly, but can also be clarified quickly. This Tarot card is nothing less than a mirror image of your relationship: lightning bolts are still flying, but a rainbow shimmers, and the sparkling crystal heralds the emerging clarity.

Be aware of the worth of your relationship, and take care that communication is open between you and your beloved. If you have had quarrels, now is a good time to set them aside. Misunderstandings can be resolved and doubts removed.

What is required for this to happen is that you deal clearly and directly with each other. Don't say, »Well, if it's right for you and your headache is gone, since it wasn't bad last time, it would probably be good for you if, on this beautiful full-moon night, we, maybe, did something together again«. Just say, »I'd like to sleep with you tonight«.

It's also important not to let your partner make demands on you. Your friendship will be strengthened if you set limits for yourself and represent your point of view clearly.

Question: *What do you and your partner need to clarify?*

Suggestion: *Talk with your partner about how you are doing now, what concerns and touches you at the moment. Be honest, open, and direct.*

Affirmation: *Through my directness and openness I bring clarity into my relationship.*

Nine of Wands – Strength

Key Words: *Healing; strength; growth; purification; becoming aware of old wounds; connectedness; expansion.*

Healing is now possible between you and your partner. The possibility for healing arises because you can now shed light on all areas of your relationship which have lain hidden in darkness until now. The process of perceiving may be painful, but remember that it serves your inner growth. A fire burns within each of you which you can use to cleanse and purify old wounds. You need only to become aware, and to enter into your pain in full awareness . These old wounds may relate to your interaction with your parents, or the death of a friend, or your own recurrent fears – whatever they are, your partner can help you now to confront what you could not, or would not see fully. You are also now in a position to do the same for your partner.

The result will be your discovery of a strength within you which you never perceived before. You will also sense an indescribable, deep feeling of connectedness with your partner. Your new-found strength and connectedness will give you the opportunity to reach beyond your own limits in all areas of life.

The dark, unconscious aspects of your partnership will become more perceivable; your increased clarity will lend you true, liberating inner strength. The entire process of setting this strength in motion may transform the quality of your relationship. You will both need a certain courage to stand by your new-found strength and implement it in the presence of your partner and others.

Question: *What are the dark areas of your relationship which you would like to become aware of with your partner?*

Suggestion: *With your partner, go to a (Rebirthing) growth group. If you already have experience in this technique, give each other a session.*

Affirmation: *Self-knowledge leads us to a full blossoming of our inner strength.*

Ten of Wands – Oppression

Key Words: *Energies held back; repressed aggressive impulses; fear of spontaneity and vitality; pressure.*

The energy created in your relationship is tremendously powerful and it invites both of you to go beyond your limits. Yet instead of setting this potential free between you, you block and repress each other. Undercurrents of fear are setting in motion certain stereotypical behavior patterns which you use to control each other. Yet in the long run you only reinforce the very thing you fear and try to hide – your aggressions.

The mutual repression of your agressive impulses creates a blockage of energies. As a result, you show yourself openly and spontaneously to your partner less and less often. If, from time to time, the pressure of your repressed feelings is released through destructive actions, you may take this as a confirmation of your idea that aggression is dangerous and must be held in check. You end by imposing even greater restrictions on your self-expression, and steering your relationship farther and farther away from love and joy.

Most of us have learned through our parents and educators to see aggression as something undesirable and dangerous. Agression is seen to be incompatible with love, harmony, and intimacy. This attitude makes it difficult to be open to this area of human emotion, especially with people we want to be close with.

The Ten of Wands shows you that this issue is pertinent to your relationship at this time. Free each other from all value judgements about what is allowed and what is not. Your aggressive impulses are natural – they are part and parcel of your life energies. The more free and accepting you can be with them, the more intelligent and creative will be your entire way of being. Only people who have made friends with their aggressive aspects and truly experience and express them, have the potential to blossom to the fullest extent possible.

Only repressed energies build up into violence and destructiveness. But your agressive potential will be expressed as love and creativity when you begin to use it constructively instead of fighting it. When you combine it with honesty, awareness, and consciousness, it can open new dimensions to you and your partner.

Your interaction will gain intensity. Even if your conflicts produce a few shards here and there, you may experience the effects of open communication as a cleansing thunder shower.

Question: *What impulses are you repressing in your relationship?*

Suggestion: *Allow yourself to act out your aggressions by yourself (screaming, hitting a pillow, etc.). Once you have let off steam, you will be more clear and open with your partner.*

Affirmation: *In open and honest expression of my aggressive impulses I experience vitality and freedom in my relationship.*

Ace of Cups

Key Words: *Cosmic, all-embracing, giving love; silence; harmony with the universe; freedom, boundlessness; tenderness, bliss, harmony, light.*

Everything is there, tenderness and bliss, silence and wonder, love and light. Of all the Minor Arcana, the Ace of Cups is closest in natur to the Major Arcana. Important aspects, such as those of the Lovers, the Sun and the Universe are contained in this card. The Ace of Cups represents love itself, love unbounded which can develop fully and totally.

You may be surprised to learn that such love is possible also in your relationship – not somewhere off in the distant future, but here and now. You now have the capacity to go beyond your personal horizon and let yourself be carried into spaces which lie outside the realm of the intellectual mind, beyond all judgements and limitations. This is a state of liberation from boundaries, a state of great openness.

Your relationship is not the center but the starting point. Cosmic love can develop from your deep love for each other. You can both feel the fine fibers of light binging you to each other and the universe. New dimensions may open for you, and you may gain a deeper sense of your ultimate goal, the goal to which your love leads you together.

Question: *When you are with a beloved person, in what situations do you have cosmic experiences?*

Suggestion: *Make love with your partner in such a way that no physical orgasm occurs. Once your bodies are joined, reduce all movement to the minimum and become quite still. Breathe in the same rhythm, and notice that an energy field forms through the combined union of your sex and heart centers.*

Affirmation: *I am a vessel for boundless cosmic love.*

Two of Cups – Love

Key Words: *Love; receptiveness; fulfilled love relationship; completeness; union; harmonious togetherness; deep surrender.*

You have arrived at a beautiful sea of harmony and love. In your relationship, moments of stillness and complete union with your beloved are possible; moments which all people yearn for in their lives.

The Two of Cups tells you that such moments can become reality in your life. You don't need a perfect partner – something that doesn't exist anyway. This kind of love makes no demands or prerequisites for the other. It demonstrates an inner willingness toward unselfish and total surrender to the mystery of love.

For this to occur, you need a deep sense of self-love. Only those who accept themselves totally can open themselves fully for another. The love we wish to give to others must first be born and developed in ourselves, toward ourselves.

You can receive a great deal from your partner, and this card encourages you to accept it. Whoever wants to give must first learn to receive. No service is expected from you in return, no big demonstrations, and no proofs of your love. If you are open and trust your partner, this is enough. You can enjoy the wealth of your emotions together. Your love is real. You can let yourself be guided by it into previously unknown depths. On the way, do nothing else except to remain aware, and celebrate your aliveness.

Question: *What helps you experience love for yourself and for your partner?*

Suggestion: *Find a gift for your partner which expresses your love in a special way.*

Affirmation: *I surrender to love.*

Three of Cups – Abundance

Key Words: *Love; trust; closeness; emotional wealth; intensity; interchange; surrender.*

There is a very valuable secret which you and your partner share only with each other. It is something unique. Be aware of this secret, and if you don't know it is there, look for it now.

The Three of Cups indicates a special point of light in your relationship. You and your partner can share some particularly rare and valuable feelings and perceptions. You may find them in your sexual expression, in meditation together, or in conversation and verbal interchange.

The basic message is: you have an abundance of everything necessary for your relationship and yourselves to flourish and develop. You have nothing to do but to accept gratefully the gifts being showered upon you. You, in turn, have a great deal to give to your partner simply by being just the way you are.

This card often indicates the presence of a third person that you are close to as a couple. You can now expand and deepen your relationship with this person.

Question: *What is that specialness between you?*

Suggestion: *Take an evening to share something of great value with each other.*

Affirmation: *I enjoy the overflowing richness in my relationship.*

Four of Cups – Luxury

Key Words: *Love, care, attention, motherliness; familiarity; danger of restrictions or limitations resulting from excessive care.*

You receive from your partner and he or she receives from you a great deal of love. This is a part of your emotional wealth which expresses itself in your relationship through generosity, luxury, and beauty. You can share inner richness with your partner as with few other people.

The attentiveness of your partner has a great deal to do with motherliness and care for your welfare. This awakens a sort of primal trust in your relationship. This trust allows you to dive into the depths of your souls. The more consciously you deal with your feelings, the more you can accept and give them. Rejoice in your togetherness, but don't restrict or limit yourselves to only that. Your relationship can remain vital only if you share your emotional wealth with other peoples as well.

The card »Luxury« also warns you never to let yourself give up your independence in return for an excess of emotional caring. In times of luxury, you must be doubly alert. Especially in very familiar or close and intimate relationships, too much caring for each other's welfare can become oppressive. In terms of the image on the card, the heavens of clarity can become darkened, and the water of the emotions loses its purity.

Question: *Do you or your partner tend to restrict or limit the other through excessive caring or devotion?*

Suggestion: *Give your partner a day on which you will mother him or her: bring breakfast in bed, read a story out loud, cook something delicious, caress and coddle your partner. On a different day, let yourself be mothered by your partner. Exchange your impressions and feelings about the experience of both roles.*

Affirmation: *I enjoy our emotional wealth in freedom.*

Five of Cups – Disappointment

Key Words: *Disappointment; unrealistic expectations; disillusionment; discontent; sadness.*

When you draw the Five of Cups, it usually indicates old emotional wounds from earlier relationships which are now being felt again in an equally painful way. What your partner is now bringing up in you may reach far into the primal experiences of your early childhood. Your beloved's behavior is calling up and awakening in you long forgotten feelings of fear and disappointment which you may have thought you had overcome and resolved. You feel helpless and at the mercy of these emotions.

Rather than accusing the other, be aware that you are in an important phase of emotional cleansing and healing. Your partner has taken on a meaningful role in this process. Because of your earlier disappointments, you may tend to project your own frustrated needs onto your partner. But whoever seeks the perfect partner is bound to be disappointed. You have to learn that you will find your own fulfillment only within yourself, never outside yourself. If you continue to seek emotional security in others as you did when you were a child needing your parents, you merely express your lack of responsibility to and for yourself, and your poor sense of independence. The fear of disappointment is always based in inappropriate, infantile expectations which can not be fulfilled until you recognize your own lackings and accept them.

Every disappointment is based on self-deception. Begin now to stand by your own personal desire and needs without expecting your partner to fulfill them. Once you have made this very important step toward yourself, you will have learned the essential lesson of this Tarot card.

Question: *Which areas of your own neediness and expectations are you hiding from your partner out of your of disappointment?*

110

Suggestion: *Write out a list with all the expectations you have of your partner, and then a second list with all the expectations you have of yourself. Read them to your partner, and talk together about them. Try especially to find out what is behind these expectations.*

Affirmation: *I stand by my needs and show them openly.*

Six of Cups – Pleasure

Key Words: *Sexuality; enjoyment; pleasure; fun with physical love; emotional interchange; the possibility to combine sex and meditation.*

The Six of Cups is the next card (after the Prince of Cups) in the Minor Arcana to place sex at the center of attention. If you draw this card, it invites you to surrender to the richness of your own emotions, your eroticism, and your sexuality. If possible, enjoy with your partner all the varieties and joy which sexual interaction offers you. There is no reason to repress yourself through irrational fears or moralistic values.

What makes sex a real pleasure is not confined only to the dimension of physical interchange. When awareness and love are added, sexuality can become the highest ecstasy. Sooner or later, this form of multidimensional love play approaches meditation.

Become more and more aware while melting together, and see how your sexuality gradually changes; see it become more still, yet more intensive, and see the physical orgasm slowly become less and less important. More than with any other means, you can heal and transform yourselves through meditative sex. If, on the other hand, your sexuality remains purely physical, you will sooner or later become bored and lose interest in each other. Give yourselves fully to the path which

111

leads deeper and deeper and becomes more and more exciting and ecstatic along the way.

Question: *Is there anything hindering you from enjoying fully your sexuality with your partner?*

Suggestion: *Buy a book about sexuality and relationships (see the suggestions for further reading at the end of this book) and read to each other from it.*

Affirmation: *I live my sexuality with awareness and love.*

Seven of Cups – Debauch

Key Words: *Negativity; over-satiety; »too much of a good thing«; sexual surfeit; boredom; old disappointments.*

Something in your relationship is »too much of a good thing«. You have probably been glued to one another too long and too closely. Whatever this »too much« might be, it serves only to divert the attention from something which is »too little« somewhere else; too little love, too little clarity, too little self confidence.

More than any other area, your sexuality is suffering from this emotional disturbance. Either very clearly, or just subliminally, you sense the surfeit with every attempt you make to regain your earlier passion and freshness. You probably need some time to be alone, so you can catch your breath in peace and quiet. This much needed space will give you the opportunity to see the emotional reality of your relationship from a new perspective, and get in touch with the actual degree of your sexual attraction to each other.

The disturbance in your relationship may also have to do with old disappointments which you have hidden away but never resolved. The more you avoid problems with your partner, the more poison collects inside you.

It is high time you started getting honest with yourself and your partner. Face up to whatever hurts you and express it. This is the only way to cleanse yourself of the poisons which, sooner or later, will threaten to corrode and consume your relationship.

Question: *Are there in your present relationship (or former ones) old disappointments which you have not expressed to your partner?*

Suggestion: *Check and see if you need a little space away from your partner. If so, have the courage to give it to yourself.*

Affirmation: *I cleanse myself of everything which disturbs my relationship to myself and my partner. I stand by myself and my feelings one hundred percent.*

Eight of Cups – Indolence

Key Words: *Stagnation; emotional swamp; lack of power, loss of energy; indolence, lack of drive; indifference, dullness, gloominess; numbness, paralysis; mutual sucking dry.*

The Eight of Cups shows that the energy flow between you and your partner is at a standstill. The honeymoon is long gone. The feelings that onde drew you together and were a source of intensity, pleasure, and enjoyment have lost their vitality. They have evolved into a colorless, stagnant side-by-side existence. Being together with your partner no longer arouses feelings of joy in life as it once did. Instead it sucks you dry of your last ounce of energy and drive.

You try vainly again and again to revitalize your relationship, but your well-meant efforts find no resonance. Powerless and empty, you are left standing face to face with your emotional stagnation. The more you try to revive your stalled situation, the more defeated you feel. Your attempts to revive your partner leak and trickle away into the stagnant water of your unexpressed emotions.

It is high time that you remembered your own autonomy. That means learning to set clear limits and learning to say »no«. You have already wasted too much energy on people who gave nothing back to you. They were bottomless containers which you had hoped to fill with your care.

This may be an old behavior pattern of yours – always to direct your love toward people who give nothing in return. In using this behavior, you can avoid your own fears of being loved. Your partners always live up to your own structures. They also are avoiding deep and real closeness. At the same time, everyone is afraid of being left alone. Many couples stew in their swampy relationships together because neither of them has learned to find fulfillment in him or her self.

Your task right now is to look very carefully at the lessons you have to learn with each other, and then come to the appropriate conclusions. Your relationship may just be a framework for your old self-imposed limitations: then separate from your partner. But maybe this particular partner is presenting you with the opportunity to recognize your mechanical behavior patterns and to go beyond them: then realize that your own lack of consciousness has helped to influence your partner's behavior. In this, as in every situation, the same rule applies – the other is never responsible for you!

Question: *In which situations do you paralyze and weaken each other?*

Suggestion: *From now on, say »no« to whatever you do not really want. Talk with your partner about everything which makes you feel confined and inhabited.*

114

Affirmation: *I rediscover my independence. Now I have the strength and courage to set my own limits and say »no«.*

Nine of Cups – Happiness

Key Words: *Harmony; happiness; bliss; strong radiance; openness; permeability; joyful sharing.*

You live in a true house of joy. Much more is possible between you and your beloved than just the superficial touching of two bodies; in your togetherness arises harmony. As soon as you allow your energy and feelings to flow freely, they will complement each other and bring forth a melody like no other in the universe.

When this happens, sensitive people will feel drawn to you and will rejoice in you and with you. The happiness depicted in the Nine of Cups has a quality of openness, as well as one of celebration and sharing. It springs from an overflowing love whose ecstatic expression touches all who are open to it. It has a tendency to draw others closer and infest them too. This joy can rise in you without any visible external cause. It strives for expression, and you feel as if you could embrace the whole world.

In fact, th Nine of Cups represents an exchange of joy which must not be restricted to just you and your partner. What you are sharing with your beloved is something you would like to share with many others. It becomes your state of being, from which everyone who is open to it can receive. Everyone who resonates with you will increase and deepen your own happiness.

Question: *What beliefs and behavior patterns hinder your joy, and which increase it?*

Suggestion: *Be involved with your partner in groups which allow you to share and celebrate your togetherness with other open and receptive people.*

Affirmation: *Happiness fills my being. In open exchange with other people I find my fulfullment.*

Ten of Cups – Satiety

Key Words: *Fulfillment; satisfaction; sharing with other people; overflowing love; radiance.*

The Tree of Life, with its ten cups, depicts a state of fulfillment and satisfaction, of harmony and equilibrium. The fiery warlike energy of Mars is totally unified with the gentle water energy of Pisces.

The frictions and struggles which went on in your relationship were not in vain. They were present in order to guide your polarities together in a fruitful and creative way. This complementation of your energies gives rise to a new quality in your togetherness.

When you open deeply to each other, you also become able to share your new qualities lovingly and generously with other people. You should open up beyond the familiar boundaries of your own partnership.

Each of you has gained enough inner strength in your relationship to be loving and empathetic, clear and powerful, weak and vulnerable with others.

There is nothing special to **do**, you simply need to **be** wherever and however you are at the moment. Your love for your partner leads you to universal love which arises from the whole and knows no limitations.

Question: *What are the polarities between you and your partner which enrich your relationship?*

Suggestion: *Seek opportunities, either with or without your partner, in which you can share the emotional richness you have found in your relationship with other people.*

Affirmation: *I radiate the love which I have received.*

Ace of Swords

Key Words: *Clarity; honesty; directness; uncompromising; expanded perception; flawlessness.*

Flawlessness and unimpeachable clarity are the attributes of The Ace of Swords. This represents a tremendous opportunity for you and your partner to come clean with each other and enter a purified state. You have an ability now to see things very clearly, so you are also able to grasp the deeper implications of what is happening in your situation. You are free of illusions, so you have the courage to see things as they are and »to call a spade a spade«.

Your task and the responsibility involved are not always easy. Recognition of the truth exposes and destroys illusions. This makes it impossible for you to continue on the old paths of half-heartedness and cowardice. You can no longer kid yourself or your partner without realizing that you are compromising your own inner truth.

This means you must be carful to keep the clarity of your perceptions in intimate contact with the voice of your heart and your love. If you do so, you will sense your partner being able to accept and take a great deal from you. What you communicate to your partner will be free of accusations and attempts to manipulate or hurt your beloved.

Clarity will begin to pervade not only your words, but also your behavior and your entire aura. It will surround you like a light to reveal the shadows of unawareness, robbing them of their power to delude. Even if you have to express truths which may be painful and difficult for your partner to hear, your loving honesty will open the paths toward greater awareness for you both.

Question: *In which ways do you bring clarity into your relationship?*

118

Suggestion: *Take this time to express and clarify everything in your relationship which has been floating unspoken and unacknowledged between you.*

Affirmation: *I share my perceptions openly and lovingly with my partner.*

Two of Swords – Peace

Key Words: *Peace; clarity; insight; decisiveness; meditation; time for silence.*

All cares and conflicts which have attracted your attention in your partnership can now be put to rest. This card offers great clarity bound together with true inner peace and deep stillness. Something in you is now open to that state which no one can create yet which sometimes comes upon you in unexpected moments and situations. This often happens in the midst of the chaos of your thoughts and emotions – a moment of pause, of sudden remembrance and clarity. In this state you are no longer bound by external demands – you see your own reality and your partner's reality in a new light. When you draw this card, you express your great openness to such an experience.

You may not always succeed in getting your partner to share in this experience. But this is no problem for you. True peace allows you and your partner freedom and the space each needs to have his or her own experiences. If possible, do invite your partner to meditate with you. If your partner agrees, the shared meditations will be your most appropriate means of communicating. Give yourselves a time for stillness. The gifts which will grow out of it for both of you are immeasurably valuable.

The card »Peace« also indicates that a good time is here in your relationship to come to decisions and, if necessary, to clarify any tensions. You don't need to fight. Your inner strength and intuition will help you through this process. If you know yourself, your decisions will create inner peace. This sense of inner peace will come when your decisions give rise to behavior patterns that create movement in your relationship.

Question: *Are there any decisions that need to be made concerning your partner?*

Suggestion: *Allow yourself a time of stillness and meditation with your partner. Afterwards, talk with your partner about whatever decisions need to be made in regard to your relationship.*

Affirmation: *I share my clarity and my peace with my partner.*

Three of Swords – Sorrow

Key Words: *Sorrow; cares; fear of loss; jealousy; difficult triangular relationship; necessity for meditation.*

Your relationship is causing you sorrow. You are worried about your shared existence. This can touch on many different aspects of your relationship, but one is especially affected – the fear of losing your partner.

Such fears are often based on actual realities in a relationship, but they are also often based on irrational reasons. Your partner may have inwardly turned from you recently, and you have to struggle for attention or affection from him or her. Or a third person has broken into your relationship, calling into question all your accustomed or habitual behaviors and shaking the two of you widely awake.

Hand in hand with the fear of losing your partner comes the old theme of jealousy. It must be dealt with honestly and carefully now. Because just about everyone is faced with jealousy at one time or another, we have come to accept it as the normal reaction. In fact, if someone reacts other than with possessiveness and jealousy, we assume that person doesn't really love at all. Love only seems real to us when the other tries to chain us to him or herself.

While it is important for us to accept and admit to our own feelings of jealousy, it is equally important for us to see that what is in us, trying to hold and cling to the other, is never love.

»It is not love, which is jealous. See it in yourself, observe it again and again ... just as the sun knows nothing of darkness, love knows nothing of jealousy. Jealousy is possessiveness, hate, rage, violence, it is made up of a multitude of things, but never of love. Because all these things are so ugly, they can not exist without masks.

Love is only possible when meditation has happened. If you don't know how you can rest in your own center, if you don't know how you can relax and rest in your own being, if you don't know how to be alone and blissful, then you will never know what love is.

Love appears like relationship to something, but it arises from a deep loneliness. Love expresses itself in relations, but the source, the spring of love is in meditation.« (Bhagwan Shree Rajneesh, **Love Starts after the Honeymoon**, Rajneesh-Services Verlag, Cologne, W. Germany)

Jealousy is nothing to be ashamed of. The degree to which we are jealous indicates the degree to which we tend to use other people to separate ourselves from ourselves. Jealousy contains, therefore, a reminder to concentrate on ourselves again.

Jealousy is always rooted in a comparison between ourselves and our rival. The more we accept and love ourselves, the more the patterns which drive us to such behavior simply disappear. When we have a deep knowledge of our own worth, even the pain of losing someone who is important to us merely guides us to greater and deeper awareness. The power to go deeper comes from our love of ourselves.

Question: *How do you deal with your jealousy?*

Suggestion: *Talk with your partner about your jealousy. Describe how it feels to you. Then describe situations in which you become jealous. Try, together with your partner, to discover the causes of your jealousy.*

Affirmation: *In accepting my jealousy, I find my way back to myself.*

Four of Swords – Truce

Key Words: *Temporary retreat; taking your own space; warning to douse smoldering conflicts.*

Right now, neither hard fighting nor great love scenes are appropriate between you and your partner. The most important thing for you is to create a little space for each other so you can both breathe. Instead of rushing to make decisions, retreat into your own center. As soon as you have achieved clarity within, you can bring clarity into your relationship.

A temporary retreat helps you see your relationship from a different perspective. This may sometimes be a sobering experience, but it also broadens your horizons. When you get together with your partner later, you will find more intensity between you than if you had spent the entire time glued to each other.

Truce also indicates danger. In every relationship, certain agreements, unspoken contracts and arrangements are made which stabilize and shield the relationship. They can also, however, be used to sweep disagreements and conflicts under the rug. This card warns you not to let conflicts which are smoldering below the surface to continue unabated. The surface may look smooth and fine, but a time-bomb is ticking not far below. Only if you recognize this bomb and de-fuse it in time you can avoid destructive arguments and allow constructive interchange to take place.

Question: *Are there any unspoken agreements in your relationship which help you avoid conflict?*

Suggestion: *Talk openly with your partner about whatever you feel is oppressing you, but you never dared discuss before. Talk about your hidden fears, your unexpressed annoyance, etc.*

Affirmation: *Through openness we attain clarity.*

Five of Swords – Defeat

Key Words: *Loss – Fear; defensive aggression; flight; hiding one's true feelings; fear of defeat and betrayal.*

You are afraid of losing – of losing control, your partner, your ego. Out of fear, you either attack or flee into your snail shell. At the same time, your swords bend, and the attack aims at you. You alone are responsible for your wounds, against which you so desperately try to defend yourself.

Someone who draws this card may, for example, harbor the plan to leave the relationship out of fear that the partner will leave. To avoid pain, you try to second guess. You run away before you are chased away, you strike before you are struck, you give up before you struggle in vain, you withdraw because in your thoughts defeat seems much too threatening and inevitable. At the same time, you often fail to recognize how much you are robbing yourself, how you are slowly bleeding yourself dry.

You could also use your energies creatively, rather than directing them toward your fear. Whether your fears are justi-

123

fied or not becomes clear only when you risk something, and when you lay yourself open to life and to your partner. Usually you will find out how unfounded your terrifying fantasies were. But even if you are actually defeated, you still have the choice to accept with dignity and learn from it. In every defeat lies a hidden victory.

Question: *In your relationship, what would »defeat« mean?*

Suggestion: *Both you and your partner will need two pieces of paper. On one, write down what the other has done to hurt you recently. On the second piece, write down what you think you have done to hurt the other. When you are finished, read your ideas to each other and talk about him.*

Affirmation: *I openly show my partner my fears and worries.*

Six of Swords – Science

Key Words: *Readiness to communicate; mutual inspiration; powers of thought; understanding; fruitful intellectual interchange.*

In a relationship the card Science indicates intellectual interchange. See this as a valuabel area of your togetherness. Each of you is able to inspire the other and move on to new and interesting realizations.

For a man and woman in a love relationship, this level of interaction becomes, in time, unsatisfying (although there are exceptions that prove the rule). If your interaction is too rational, reasonable and intellectual, your relationship may become somewhat cool and distant. The plane of thoughts alone encompasses only specific and limited areas. Vitality, emotionality, and physicality should also always be given enough space for expression.

If you have the feeling that the mental and verbal interaction is getting the shorter end in your relationship, this card is a positive hint to give this area more attention than in the past.

You may not always be of the same opinion, but you can develop the capacity to bring your different perspectives to a common point. The ideas of one can enrich the mental world of the other. If you examine and uncover your shared process analytically, you can get to know each other better by understanding each other. If you let your points of view come together, something new and even greater can crystallize from them.

In order for this exchange to occur on deeper planes, you have to be prepared to »get into your partner's head«. You have to view your partner's thoughts and ideas as if they were your own. At the same time, you need to be open to letting your own ideas grow and change. Let your beloved inspire you – and you will discover brand new petals on the rose of realization.

Question: *Does your relationship need more interchange on the mental level?*

Suggestion: *Take two or more hours in order to understand each other completely, to get into each other's heads. Then play the role of your partner while your partner plays you. Talk and behave as you believe the other would. While being your partner, express the fears and desires you believe he or she has. At the end, talk about what you experienced. You have a chance to make some pretty exciting discoveries and have some stimulating experiences with this game.*

Affirmation: *I understand and am understood.*

Seven of Swords – Futility

Key Words: *Doubt; negative expectations; despondency; insecurity; a feeling of weakness.*

A moment ago you were completely calm and clear, but in the next instant your doubts rose up again, loudly baying at your heels like a pack of hounds. »Does she really love me?« »Am I really enough for him?« »Why we used to sleep together more frequently than now?« and so on. While such thoughts are shooting trough your mind, you lose your view of reality.

You should accept your relationship as it is here and now, instead of constantly thinking what may or might happen in the »there and then«. Doubt and negative expectations are the only dangers now threatening your togetherness. You can banish these dangers by awakening and perceiving reality.

If you are not prepared to do so, the destructive force of your thoughts will, sooner or later, bring about the very events you claim to fear the most.

If you look inside yourself deeply and honestly, you have to realize that you are never just a victim of circumstance. You seek out and create the so-called negative yourself. You expectations, either conscious or subconscious, attract corresponding events because you need these events to help you awaken. If you understand this simple fact, you can relax and accept thankfully whatever life happens to offer or take away.

Doubts about your relationship always arise from your deepest self-doubts, so you must first shed light on your own internal workings. If your fail to do this, you sand to repeat the same disappointing experiences in all your relationships.

Question: *What negative dogmas are the basis of your fear?*

Suggestion: *Speak openly with your partner about all your questions and doubts. Test your shared reality. Tell each other* *honestly all your secret wishes and fears. If you cannot do this with your partner, write it out for yourself.*

Affirmation: *I always get what I need most. I accept gratefully whatever is given to or taken from me in my relationship.*

Eight of Swords – Interference

Key Words: *Mistrust; ambivalence; fear of making the wrong decisions; brooding; top-heaviness; uncertainty.*

Your relationship at this time is ruled more by the head or mental aspect, which leaves it more open to disturbances and disruption than usual. You don't dare do be honest with your partner, so your relationship is lacking in clarity. The situation demands a decision from you, but that is exactly what scares you the most.

You feel torn and search in vain for a solution. But the more you think about it, the less secure the ground beneath you seems to be.

As long as you only reflect and think, without feeling your own inner truth, you will remain trapped in this vicious cycle. You can only escape by letting your energy go down from the head to the heart.

The actual disturbing factor in your relationship is you. It may be, however, that someone from »outside« is actually interfering as well. Maybe one of you is thinking about whether things would be better back with the former partner, or whether he or she just let a chance go by with someone else . . . Such mind games, which can easily become a form of self-torment, don't help on your relationship. The Eight of Swords – Interference – does not indicate a change of partners right now.

You will be better off letting things rest and develop on their own. Maybe new aspects will develop which you cannot foresee. This is not really a time for decisions, but a time to regain your inner clarity and warmth of heart.

Question: *What aspects of your relationship demand a decision?*

Suggestion: *Sit opposite your partner, hold hands, and look at each other. Breathe through your noses for ten minutes. Breathe deeply, and direct your breath toward the abdomen. Maintain eye-contact the entire time! After ten minutes, give your bodies room the move without controlling them. Afterwards, express your impressions and experiences without interpreting or judging.*

Affirmation: *I relax and find my clarity.*

Nine of Swords – Cruelty

Key Words: *Self hatred; sneering; thoughtlessness, brutality, cruelty, sadism; vengefulness; meanness, underhandedness; penalization; self-torment.*

»Eighty percent of all relationships are entered into so that one partner can revenge him or herself on the other.« This theory, stated by the reincarnation therapist Chris Griscom, is, at this time, meaningful in your situation. The Nine of Swords shows up a tendency in you to do yourself and your partner harm in some way. You hurt yourself and your partner to such a degree that your relationship is put into extreme jeopardy.

Cruelty in relationships points to a tendency of one partner to put himself down in comparison to the other. This is expressed in many forms of self-torment, self-accusation, and self-punishment. Just as often, though, the self-hatred is projected out onto the partner, as long as the partner is open to taking on that role. That partner then becomes the scape goat to have

128

accusations, sneering jibes and verbal abuse heaped on his or her head. This can escalate into the most brutal forms of physical and mental violence.

When you draw this card in regard to your relationship, you have to find out if it points to your own self-hatred, or to the cruelty you are either expressing or receiving from the outside. Usually all three are involved, each to a different degree.

Very often, there are old wounds. Either you are poking around in them, or someone else is. You are punishing yourself in the ways your parents did. Or maybe you hit your partner with the blow of a sword because at one time you would have liked to hit your parents that way, but never did.

Your task right now is to feel your pain and to let your partner see it. In addition, you need to learn to recognize the patterns which are the basis of your self-torment and cruel behavior. This is the only way things can change. Partnership and cruelty don't mix – they always lead to destruction and isolation.

If your drawing of this card about your present partner surprises you, look very carfully at the subtle layers of your own self-negation. Cruelty doesn't always express itself obviously or dramatically. There may be important parts of yourself, or aspects of your relationship, which you would prefer to deny, or which, for some reason, you cannot easily forgive.

Question: *Have you forgiven yourself, your parents, your present, and former partners for current and past mistakes?*

Suggestion: *Take 30 minutes to write down everything you find negative about yourself and your partner. Then read your lists to each other and discuss them.*

Affirmation: *I forgive myself and others for current and past mistakes and failings by recognizing and understanding them.*

Ten of Swords – Ruin

Key Words: *Fear of insanity; self-hatred; disillusionment; destroyed relationship; sense of meaninglessness; wounds; the end.*

When you draw the Ten of Swords, expressions like, »crazy with fear«, or »You're going to drive my crazy«, have become more than mere phrases for you. This card reflects your entire negativity, your self-hatred, your fear of going crazy.

The areas of your relationship that were founded on illusions are losing their apparent solidity and are breaking apart like a house of cards. You are afraid to admit this is happening because you fear the downfall of your shared (unconscious) lies and the resultant chaos.

Your relationship has reached its absolute lowest point. Your hearts are wounded and neither of you sees a way out of the rubble heap which is all that remains of your ideals. A barren, empty desert is all that is left of the paradise your relationship once might have been. At this point, most couples choose one of the following two options. They either separate, or they rearrange themselves and continue to vegetate like cacti in the desert of their relationship – demanding nothing, and full of prickly spikes.

You have, however, a third possibility. You can choose to go through this low point together. To do so, you will need courage, daring to take risks, and honesty. You have to learn once again to be vulnerable and to show this vulnerability. You also have to learn to look honestly at your fears and recognize them for what they are: projections. Get up very close to the screen on which you are projecting your terrifying images and you will see that the screen is just an innocent white surface. You can turn your ruin, your »downfall« into a dive into new depths, if you are prepared to say »yes« to life, »yes« to your fear, and »yes« to your love.

Question: *What illusions in your relationship have become shaky now?*

Suggestion: *For one (or more) day(s), don't say one word to each other, and, if possible, speak very little to anyone else. Whenever you feel fear during this period of time, write it down. After a few days, read your »fear-notes« to each other, and talk about them and anything else you have experienced in the silent period.*

Affirmation: *I am now ready to recognize and let go of my illusions.*

Ace of Disks

Key Words: *Inwardly and outwardly richt; fulfillment; great success; inner strength; shared growth; unity of matter and spirit, physicality and spirituality.*

Now, between you and your partner, a kind of union is possible which is far more all-embracing than you have thought. Physicality and spirituality, love and stillness, yin und yang – now you can allow all these to melt together in complete harmony.

The Ace of Disks shows a time of all-embracing fulfillment for you and your relationship. The material and spiritual planes unite in a harmonious whole. Inward and outward richness, a state of natural and boundless being, can now characterize your relationship with your beloved. Now is a time of celebration, enjoyment and fulfillment on all planes.

Your relationship stands on solid ground. Even crisis or conflicts will not really shake you. They will simply help you to sift out everything that is superfluous in your relationship so you can go ever deeper. You have a chance to arrive at a new level of consciousness.

In your connection with your beloved, your own inner beauty becomes more and more apparent. Your partner's presence encourages the development of your potential, and helps you give more definite expression to your abilities and strengths.

In general, the circumstances are such that you can both be more inwardly intensive and more outwardly free. Joint projects of every kind promise great success, whether they are focused toward earning money or attending a spiritual growth group. You have found each other to support each other in the full development of your internal and external riches.

Question: *In which areas of your relationship do you find the most fulfillment. How can you both extend this into other areas?*

Suggestion: *Travel to some place you always wanted to go, and spend a weekend of love there. Or, go together to a weekend session of the group »Inner and Outer Wealth« (described at the end of this book).*

Affirmation: *In togetherness with my beloved I develop my inner and outer richness.*

Two of Disks – Change

Key Words: *New enterprises; internal and external changes; rarely, a change of partners; progress together; transformation.*

Every relationship can blossom and remain vital only if the partners are open to constant change, for new suggestions, for examination, and analysis, and for basic alterations.

Allow things to change. If you have drawn this card, the time has come for you to be open to new things in your relationship. If you have no partner, be ready to meet one.

If you are already in a relationship, be ready to move forward with your partner into new realms of your togetherness. This can, in rare cases, indicate a change in the form of a new partner approaching you. However, this card usually points to a change within an existant relationship. The change will be a fundamental one.

This can simply mean that you will look for a place to live together, that you are prepared to enter into a project together, that you will travel together, or that in some way you will change your relationship. The fact is, we often choose external changes to encourage and support internal change. If this is not the case for you, you will eventually be left feeling dissatisfied and drained by your search for external change alone. Allow the change to become a solid basis for your inner and outer growth; let it be your launching pad to new hights.

Question: *What was the last big change in your relationship with your partner? What changes which you can imagine now cause you the most fear?*

Suggestion: *Sit together with your partner. Close your eyes and each of you imagine what changes in your relationship would be the greatest challenge for you. After a while, open your eyes, and tell each other what you have pictured, fantasized. Tell each ohter your fears, and what parts of your fantasies you would like to realize.*

Affirmation: *I am open for internal and external change in my relationship with my partner.*

Three of Disks – Works

Key Words: *Work on relationship; confrontation with the daily routine; clearing out, attaining clarity; gradual progress.*

If you want to go into the depths through your relationship, you have to let yourself go wholeheartedly. This means also going into the daily routine. A deep relationship does not only comprise heated weekend nights; conflicts, cares, misunderstandings, arguments, and annoyance can be part of it too.

The Three of Disks challenges you to confront the more difficult aspects of your partner as well. Don't let yourself be overwhelmed by the routine or problems that arise. Try to recognize them with awareness and clarify things. Two things that can help you in this are meditaion done together at certain times and regular discussions about all areas which are problematic.

Whatever you have to work through in your relationship now demands the complete and total commitment of your mental, physical, and spiritual powers. If you enter into this with all your energies, you will be richly rewarded by the gradual progress in your relationship. This is not the time for great leaps forward. This is the time for you to commit yourself to achieving the clarity needed now in your realtions with your partner. You may sometimes find this arduous and taxing. But if you now give your undivided attention to the needs of the moment, what you sow will reward you sooner or later with a bountiful harvest. Go step by step, and take into consideration everything which life demands of you in regard to your relationship.

The care you take now with your partner will be well worth the effort. Life and love can only blossom, if you have prepared the ground carefully for them.

Question: *Are you internally prepared to take on also the difficult and mundane aspects of your relationship?*

Suggestion: *Do the »Dynamic Meditation« together with your partner. (Cassettes and instructions available in bookshops.)*

Affirmation: *In opening myself to all dimensions of our relationship, I come close to myself and my partner.*

Four of Disks – Power

Key Words: *Power games, tests of power; rigid structures; oppression; protective walls; reliability, strenght; ability to »build» on each other.*

In many relationships it looks as if one partner loves the other more than he or she is loved in return. Perhaps one looks strong and independent while the other appears weak and needy. If there is a stronger and a weaker one in your relationship, your game of love has been reduced to a game of power.

This card challenges you to see these power games and let go of them. Stop putting your partner under pressure – either by ordering him or her around, or by constant complaining, or by playing the helpness one.

The Four of Disks deals with the theme of confronting power or, more generally, structures which have developed over time in your relationship. This card is related to the earth element, so it points up primarily material events and situations. This can concern your house and family as well as your dealings with financial matters.

Particularly in these fundamental areas, overt and/or subtle power plays are very common. If you draw this card to represent the present reality of your relationship, look very carfully at whether you are pressuring or manipulating each other through economic ties or constraints.

Some structures are useful when you are living together. Just be carful that they remain open to potential change or alteration, so that they do not become rigid principles. The sense of security you want must not be won at the expense of your vitality and freedom. Otherwise you risk making your own four walls into a prison.

Power can, however, have a positive side in loving relationships. Power indicates a tremendous energy potential in your relationship. Once you overcome your fears and mistrust, once you let go to the mutual demands resulting from them, you can develop great strength together. You will be able to rely on each other and support each other. You will find that others feel comfortable and well taken care of in your presence.

Question: *Are there rigid structures in your relationship which you use to oppress each other?*

Suggestion: *Examine carefully in which ways you oppress or let yourself be oppressed by your partner. You have ten minutes in which you tell all to your partner. Express what bothers or annoys you about him or her; yell and scream if you want to. Then change places and listen to your partner. Afterwards, share* *your impressions and feelings. The exercise ends with each of your bowing down to the other and forgiving the other.*

Affirmation: *I set my power to work in the service of love.*

Five of Disks – Worry

Key Words: *a bogged-down relationship; brooding; accusations, either spoken or unspoken; feelings of guilt; routine, boredom, a stifling sense of being no more than physically next to each other, but ponderousness, blocked communication.*

In your relationship, the realm of communication and interchange is extremely blocked. You may sense that you can no longer communicate everything to your partner in the same way you once could.

Something has come between you and must be discussed and clarified openly. You may not yet be fully in touch with what it is, but deep inside you already have a sense of what areas are involved. Perhaps subconscious fear and/or guilt prevent you from fully realizing and communicating your perception to your partner. You feel isolated, and instead of engaging in an open interchange, you torment yourself with self-accussation and brooding.

You have admit that your relationship has become boring and commonplace and threatens to break up. You may certainly be able to carry on in this swampy relationship for a long time to come, but you will never be touched, let alone happy in it. If you are completly honest with yourself, you have to admit you cannot continue this way.

Your only chance is to communicate with your partner openly, without misguided consideration for his or her feelings, even if the task seems very difficult. Talk together and hold back nothing. Prepare now to seek new paths, and be open to walking them with or without your present companion.

In any case, the important thing for you is to become active and take the initiative. If you take the chance and let go of old forms of relating, the problem of your present situation can become an opportunity for you to free yourself.

Question: *What is weighing on your mind which you don't dare clarify with your partner?*

Suggestion: *Do an active meditation with your partner, for example, the »Dynamic Meditation«. Afterwards, sit down together and talk about whatever has been standing between you unexpressed.*

Affirmation: *I am now ready to hold openly and honestly to my own needs.*

Six of Disks – Success

Key Words: *Success; happy outlook; harmony; rich potential in your togetherness.*

Your partnership promises success on all levels, in all areas. The inner wealth which binds you together can manifest itself now in many external realms. Joint undertakings promise successful outcomes. Everything you take on together is supported by the whole. The six planets come to your side with their advice.

Saturn: Even in this phase of success, accept the existing structures. They will help you remain centered even in the midst of your overwhelming joy.

Jupiter: This is just the beginning! This success with your partner indicates that your good fortune and happiness has no set boundaries.

Venus: Let your hearts guide you. Grace, beauty, and emotional interchange should accompany you and your shared path.

Moon: When you trust your intuition and let your joint efforts spring from the basis of your intuitions and perceptions, your external success will also satisfy and fulfill your inner realms.

Mercury: Be open in exchanging your ideas and thoughts. Share your wealth generously with others.

Mars: Never hesitate to do that which arises from your own innermost selves. Be ready to face your internal resistances without fear. Make no lazy compromises. Existing conflicts can be easily overcome now. In your togetherness with this partner you experience a harmony which corresponds to your deepest being. This freedom from tension and disturbance is to be accepted and enjoyed gratefully. By taking on this success with great awareness, you create an openness inside yourselves which will attract other gifts from existence.

Question: *Is there something you would like to undertake with your partner now?*

Suggestion: *Share your plans and ideas with your partner. Your chances for shared success are very good.*

Affirmation: *I enjoy thankfully the gift of our success.*

Seven of Disks – Failure

Key Words: *Fear of loss; fear of failure; lack of self confidence; inhibitions; negative expectations; repressed fears.*

The fear of failure with your partner relates most strongly to the material/physical plane. Depending on the actual situation, it can arise in various areas. It can be the fear of failing in your sexual relations, the fear of not being attractive enough for your partner, or not being able to satisfy your partner. It can also be a fear of impotence or frigidity. This card also often points out general fears about loss.

A physical separation would bring about the loss of emotional nourishment and support, and perhaps also the loss of financial support. You may also fear failure in a joint business venture or enterprise, or you may be worried about your health and vitality.

If love really flows between you and your partner, why are you afraid to fail or be unable to fulfill certain expectations? The basis of a deep relationship is trust, and that is what you are lacking now. You and your partner should look together at your fears. See what you are afraid of (or what both of you are afraid of) and lay out your worst possible scenarios. Then tell each other just how real your negative expectations are. Be aware that unwanted events come upon you because you expect and thus attract them. Look back at unpleasant or bad experiences in your own lives. Remember what you were thinking, feeling, and doing before these things happened.

As soon as you recognize and understand your fear, you can also let go of it and replace it with positive expectations. Whether you have a partner now or not is of no importance. The point is for you to increase your own self-confidence and self-trust, for example with affirmations. Once you have done so, your fear of failure can quickly turn into joy in success.

Question: *In which areas do you mistrust yourself or your partner? In which situations are you afraid to fail?*

Suggestion: *Falling Exercise: Put a mattress on the floor. One of you should stand with his back to the mattress, breathe deeply once or twice, and feel the fear of letting go. Wait until the moment when you are really ready to let go, and fall backwards onto the mattress. Let your voice go too, and make a sound. The other should stand to the side behind you, and catch you just before you hit the bottom.*

Affirmation: *My love and self confidence give me the power I need to master the challenges of life.*

Eight of Disks – Prudence

Key Words: *Sensitivity; tenderness; attentiveness; consideration; loving care; internal and external blossoming.*

The time for exertion and effort is past, at least for a while. Now life is blossoming, although in a very still and tender way.

Everything you need for a fulfilled love affair is there for you. The more you relax and trust that which binds you together, the more freely the beauty of your connection can develop. Be gentle and loving with your partner and yourself. However long you have been together, your relationship is a tender sapling which, at this moment, needs special care and attention.

When you go strolling through the garden which contains this sapling, leave your internal trampling elephant outside at the gate. ((In the German text, the animal mentioned is a camel – »trampeltier« literally a trampling beast. The idea is a clumsy, thoughtless animal.)) Trans. note)) Let yourself kiss the buds gently, and breathe in their fragrance as if you were touching and smelling them for the first time. Give your partner some care, even in the little things of daily life. Put a white lily in the bedroom, or make a special meal, or buy a good book as a gift.

When you are attentive and considerate with each other, you create an atmosphere in which you can grow together. Perhaps then from your tender sapling a glorious tree will grow – a tree like the one under which Buddha attained enlightenment.

Question: *Do you allow yourself and your partner the safe space necessary for the blossoming of your relationship?*

Suggestion: *Set aside a day during which you will not be disturbed by anyone, and be there completely for each other.*

Affirmation: *I relax, let go, and trust.*

Nine of Disks – Gain

Key Words: *Gain through a three-way relationship; overcoming possessiveness; open giving and receiving; union of love, creativity and intellectual exchange.*

The rosy pink disk in the center of this card shines through the green and blue ones, so that the three melt into one unity. The Nine of Disks represents the positive aspects of three-way relationships. (See also the explanations in **Tarot – Mirror of the Soul**.)

Because of jealousy and possessiveness, triangular relationships in which three people are in equally intensive and important relationships with each other are usually seen as problematic. Yet for most people it is very natural to have an intensive and complete attraction and relationship with more than one person.

142

A three-way relationship, demands a certain maturity and facility for meditative co-existence in order to succeed,. If these prerequisites are met, a triangular relationship – like that of Harris, Crowley and Regardie – can become an extremely fruitful and gainful situation.

The card Gain indicates that the same could be possible for you. Gain is also possible, and even more possible, in a three-way relationship. What is meant by gain is not the winning of a certain man or woman, but that the more you can share your love, the more you will receive. This giving must, however, come of its own accord. That means you don't limit your giving to only one person, and you give just as well if your partner is receiving not only from you but from someone else at the same time.

Three-way relationships are occasionally problematic and painful, yet they are a terrific opportunity for all involved. The effects of a third person entering into a relationship are usually enriching and bring gain to all involved.

A positive three-way relationship can also come into being when a couple decides to conceive a child. This card is not a challenge to have children, but it can indicate a need for you to come to terms with fatherhood or motherhood, especially if you already have a child.

You may be in a relationship that feels very good to you both monogamous and childless. In that case, this card is telling you to be sure that in your relationship three important elements are in harmony: love, creativity, and intellectual expression.

Question: *Have you had experience with a three-way relationship in this life? What were the gains resulting form it?*

Suggestion: *Speak openly with your partner about the people outside your relationship whom you find attractive.*

Affirmation: *I share my love openly and honestly. The more I give, the more I gain.*

Ten of Disks – Wealth

Key Words: *Wealth; ability to give; opening the relationship to the outside; unrestricted sharing with many people.*

For just a moment, let yourself feel all the treasures you bear within and those which surround you. You have infinite amounts to give to your partner, and you receive the same from him or her.

This card is reminding you how rich your relationship is, but it reminds you also not to be miserly with your wealth. So many happy couples withdraw from their friends to be there for each other alone. After a while they are forced to see that their relationship is becoming poorer and poorer, that something is missing. True wealth has to be passed on to ohters, or it becomes stale and worthless.

The possibilities of sharing with other people are limitless. You can work togehter with friends or live in a large community. You can meditate with them or go on vacation together. Give whatever you have to give, without limits, without restriction, and you will receive more in return.

If you are not fully able to share with your partner, this card is telling you, »Recognize your inner wealth, and share it with **all** the people around you. You don't need to fixate on any one person. You can be happy with anyone you like, or who is attracted to you.«

Question: *Are there any areas in your relationship in which you withhold your inner and outer wealth?*

Suggestion: *Invite serveral friends to share a lovely, festive dinner with the two of you.*

Affirmation: *I share my inner and outer wealth with all people who are open to it.*

144

6. Card Layouts and Games

Layout 1: Inner Man – Inner Woman

Everyone carries both male and female energy inside. Every man has an inner woman (anima) and every woman has an inner man (animus). Through education and societal conditioning, men have, as a rule, learned to identify themselves exclusively with their masculine side. They have the traditional role of asserting themselves in the world, where the attributes of strength, goal-orientedness, aggressivity, and/or intellectuality are assigned to them. Their feminine parts – intuition, emotions, sensitivity, and receptiveness – are thus far into the background.

On the other hand, women are expected to develop and express mainly their feminine parts – emotionality, intuition, receptiveness, and nurturing. At the same time, their intellect, their self-assertion and their capacity for action are more or less energetically repressed.

Both men and women feel incomplete, so they seek in relationships a balance for their internal imbalance. But any attempts to project their own undeveloped male or female side on an external partner are bound to lead to a dead end of disappointment and painful disillusionment.

Both sexes have to learn to find and develop those qualities they seek in partners of the opposite sex in themselves. As a woman, you should begin to give yourself and treat yourself as you would want the man of your dreams to do. As a man, you should start giving yourself everything you would like the woman of your dreams to give to you. You can only arrive at your wholeness by integrating the male and female energies within you.

The Layout:

- Sit comfortably, close your eyes, and go totally into your center. Visualize your inner man/inner woman.
- Draw from the fanned-out deck one card which will show you more about the attributes and present situation of your inner man/woman.
- Then draw a card for your external man, if you are a man, or your external woman, if you are a woman.
- You can draw cards for further question if you wish. Some example of questions you can ask are:
  »What does my inner man/woman need now?«
  »What can my external man learn from my inner woman?«
  »What can my external woman learn from my inner man?«
  »What should my inner man/woman free him/herself of?«
  »What does my inner man/woman get from my present partner?«
  »What does he/she want from my partner?«
  »What does he/she fear from my partner?«

Note: I recommend **first** answering these questions intuitively, and then drawing a card to augment and deepen your understanding.

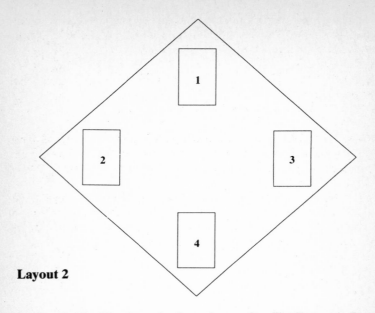

Layout 2

In-Depth Clarification of a Question or Conflict Between Partners

You can use this layout alone when you have some open questions. You can also use it together by letting one partner ask his or her questions and draw cards, and then the other.

– Mix the cards and put them in front of you in two piles. The pile on the left represents the passive receptive aspect, the one on the right represents the active, outwardly oriented aspect (like the two sides of the human body).
– Mix the pile on the left again. The top card is put in position 2 (see Fig. 1) and the bottom card is put in position 3. Lay them out face down.
– Mix the pile on the right again. Put the top card in position 1 and the bottom card in position 4.
– Uncover the cards in numerical order.

148

Card 1 shows the actual theme which is **really** occupying your thoughts now. What is the real issue? What is the basic question in relation to your partner or your relationship as a whole?

Card 2 shows what you are open and receptive for in your relationship. What energies and events are you attracting? What are you allowing to come close to you?

Card 3 tells what you show of yourself and what you give to the outer world. How do you affect your partner? What does your partner receive from you? How do you influence him/her?

Card 4 shows the answer, the key. It points out ways to resolve open questions and purify conflicts. Try new things. (Negative cards in this position show up a chance for you to put an end to a negative situation or attitude.)

Partner A

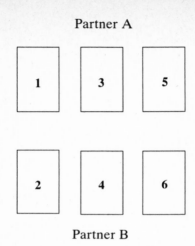

Partner B

Layout 3

Relationship Tarot

This is a simple layout to help clarify a relationship between a man and woman. It helps you find out more about the subconscious aspects, as well as about the special qualities of your connection.

You can use this game in various situations. It is good for dealing with conflicts, if both partners are prepared to see the disputed issues from a new perspective.

- Sit opposite your partner. Mix the cards one after the other. Lay them out in a fan between you.
- Take turns drawing cards and laying them face down in the following order. Lay them out accourding to Figure 2.

1. Partner A draws a card to represent him/herself.
2. Partner B draws a card to represent him/herself.
3. Partner A draws a card to represent Partner B.
4. Partner B draws a card to represent Partner A.
5. Partner A draws a card to represent the relationship.
6. Partner B draws a card to represent the relationship.

– Turn the cards over one by one, and discuss what you see!

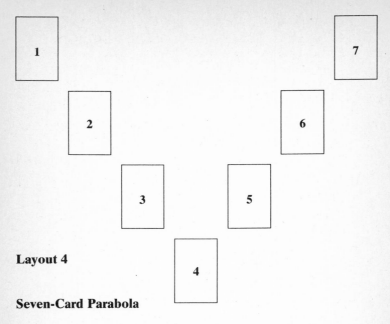

Layout 4

Seven-Card Parabola

»What should I do?« is the central question of this layout. If this question is coming up in your relationship, use this layout. You can use it alone, or with your partner. If you do it together, talk about it afterwards.

– Mix the cards and fan them out face down.
– Draw seven cards and leave them face down.
– Mix these seven cards again, and lay them out according to Figure 3.
– Turn the cards up one by one.
The cards show on the seven positions:

Card 1: The past in your relationship, or what is about to end.
Card 2: The present in your relationship.
Card 3: The future of the relationship, or what is just beginning.

Card 4: What to do.

Card 5: Helpful or disturbing influences from outside.

Card 6: Your greatest hopes and fears in regard to your partner.

Card 7: Results, outcome, key, clue to a theme which will still
concern you for a while.

Note: You can also draw the seven cards and lay them out
directly from the fanned-out deck.

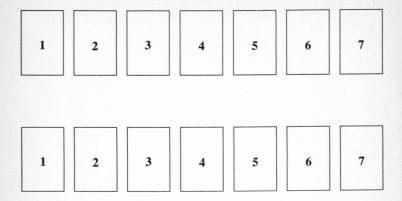

Partner A

1 2 3 4 5 6 7

1 2 3 4 5 6 7

Partner B

Layout 5

Giving and receiving

This layout helps clarify questions about the giving and receiving in a relationship. It makes clear what each is prepared to give the other and what each is withholding. It also shows up the differences between what a partner wants to give and what actually is received or needed by the other.

- The partners sit opposite each other and tune in to each other. Before mixing the cards, talk about what you give and receive from each other, and what each of your needs. While one is speaking, the other should simply listen.
- Mix the cards and fan them out.
- Take turns drawing cards. Lax them out in front of your face down in a row. Your first card should be placed opposite your partner's first card, your second opposite his or her second and so on. Draw seven cards in all (figure 4).

Card 1: A card for you.
Card 2: A card for your partner.
Card 3: I give you...
Card 4: I don't give you...
Card 5: I receive from you...
Card 6: I don't receive form you...
Card 7: I need fom you...

- Then the cards are turned up one by one; the partners discuss them.

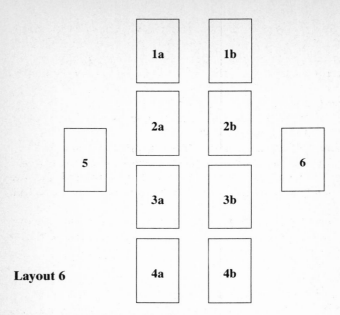

Layout 6

The Cosmic Relationship Game

This layout gives you more exact information about the motive behind your choice of partners, about the basic energy of the relationship, its main themes, and your shared tasks. This can be helpful in times of crisis – it can help you pick up the »thread« of your relationship again. But even if you are not in conflict, you can use this layout to get to know your relationship better, and to fathom the purpose of your being together.

It can be helpful to have a third person with you who knows the Tarot and can take notes.

– Sit opposite each other, look in each other's eyes a while, and tune in to each other. Both mix the cards, and then lay them out in a fan between you, face down.
– Tell each other in brief sentences or a few key words your most important impressions regarding the issues listed below.

Try to express only that which comes to your mind spontaneously at this moment. Write down a few words about each one so you can compare them with the cards you draw.

– Alternate drawing cards, and lay them out according to Figure 5.
– Each partner makes a separate layout.
– Before drawing the card for each question (1.1, 1.2, etc.), each partner should talk about it.
– At last both partners draw cards for question 5 and 6.
– Alternate turning your cards face up and comparing the card with what you said about the question beforhand. Do the two complement each other? Are there discrepancies? Talk about it!
– As you turn up each card, discuss it in comparison to the one your partner chose for the same question. How do they compare?

The Questions

1. The Motives for the relationship:
1.1. What were your **conscious motives** for entering into this relationship?
1.2. What are your conscious motives for **maintaining** this relationship?

2. The Basic Energy of the Relationship:
2.1. What was the basic energy bringing you together. What do you think was the **unconscious magnetism**?
2.2. What is the basic energy holding your relationship together now?

3. The Main Themes of the Relationship:
3.1. What are the most important **positive and supportive planes** which you share with your partner? In which areas do you understand each other and get along well?
3.2. What are the **problematic and difficult planes** in your relationship?

4. The Potential of the Relationship:
4.1. What are your joint or shared tasks in relation to inner growth and self-development.
4.2. What are your shared tasks in relation to **what you do in the world**?

5. What should be done?

6. Outlook:
What is the **theme** that will concern you both for a time to come?

Layout 7

»I love you, I hate you.«

»I love you, I hate you« is an important theme in every relationship. The following game can help you deal with it directly, and with vitality.

- The partners sit opposite each other and look into each other's eyes.
- Both mix the cards, then they fan them out between them.
- Partner A begins by verbalizing his or her feelings about Partner B. For example: »I love you.«
  »I want to live with you.«
  »I want you to be fully there for me.« etc.
- For each personal statement, A draws a card and lays it face down in order.
- B does the same. Examples:
  »I hate you.«
  »You rob me of my freedom.«
  »I am afraid of hurting you.« etc.
- Partner B also draws a card for each statement.

After both partners have said the most important things, they can begin turning up the cards.

Do the cards agree with your statements, or do they point to something quite different? Does the card for »I love you« really look like love, or the card for »I hate you« like hate? Which statements drew strong cards, which drew weak ones?

The more concretely and honestly the feelings are formulated, the more easily you will be able to approach the deeper truth behind the expressed emotions.

Layout 8

Relationship Encounter in Small Groups

Especially in small groups it can be very stimulating to clarify and explore the relationships between the members with the help of the Tarot. What is unspoken can be brought out, and people can get closer, get to know each other better, and have a good time together.

Example 1: The group sits around a table, or in a circle on the floor. The cards are laid out in the middle. One after the other, each draws a card for everyone in the group (when the group is not too large), and a card for him/herself. When everyone has drawn, the cards can be turned over, and each person spontaneously expresses what the card drawn for a particular person means in their relationship. For example,
A tells B: »With this card, I am telling you...«
A tells C: »I receive from you...« etc.
Then B tells C: »I give you in this moment...«
and so on, until all the members have heard from and talked to all the others.

Example 2: Two group members who want to clarify their relationship sit opposite each other with the cards fanned out between them. They verbalize their feelings for each other, and then use the method described under Layout 7 (»I love you, I hate you.«) to draw cards. The rest of the group gives its full attention to them and supports their attempts to clarify the relationship. This can continue until everyone has heard from and spoken with everyone else. After every pair, return the cards used to the deck and mix it again.

Layout 9

The Seven Levels

Similar to the seven chakras, or main energy centers in people, there are seven levels of relationships which you can examine with the Tarot (compare the Layout 4 »Chakra Reading« In **Tarot – Mirror of the Soul**).

When possible, do this with your partner. Starting with the lowest (root chakra) and working up to the highest (crown chakra) draw one card to represent each level.

Before doing this, read the descriptions of possible harmony or disturbance in each area. These may help you assess the situations in your relationship. Share your ideas with your partner, or write them down if doing this layout alone, before viewing each card. Then compare what you say with what the Tarot says. Are the two in agreement, or does the Tarot point up any blind spots you might have in your conscious perceptions?

Always use the Tarot with the aim of deepening your understanding of the reality of your situation. »Negative« cards indicate areas in which you and your partner have something to work through; strong »positive« cards point out the areas in which your relationship is particularly strong.

When you conduct this examination together with your partner, you may find that one partner's especially strong point falls on the same level as the other partner's especially weak or sore point. When this occurs, look carefully to see if the energy of one is living »at the expense« of the other, or if this is an area where of you have a grat deal to learn from each other.

All in all, by comparing the seven cards for each partner you will be able to recognize which areas of your relationship are free of problems and in which areas work must be done. You will see where you complement each other and are close to each other, and where there are profound differences and friction.

161

Level 1 (Root Chakra): Material co-existence

In harmony: Mutual help in career or financial support; clear and satisfying regulation of shared finances; help in matters; freedom and independence through balanced exchange; generosity in giving and receiving; shared enjoyment of material well-being, etc.

Disturbed: Financial and material dependency; pressure from debts or financial insecurity; mutual manipulation over financial matters; imbalance between giving and receiving; danger of reducing the relationship to a matter of financial security; greed and pettiness, etc.

Level 2 (Sex Chakra): The emotional-sexual connection

In harmony: Sexual attraction and fulfillment; eroticism; emotionality and admiration; physical freeness; experience of primal sexual passion; sexuality as meditation and energy transformation, etc.

Disturbed: Sexual disinterest or aversion; lack of feelings, coldness; ongoing physical disharmony and frustration; jealousy and sexual possessiveness; feelings of guilt, repulsion and self-punishment; sex as a power tool; fixing the relationship on a sexual level to compensate for a lack of love and real and deep connection; sexual enslavement, etc.

Level 3 (Solarplexus): Striving for self-assertion, achievement and power

In harmony: Mutual support for professional advancement and fulfillment of both partners; encouraging self expression of both partners; development of personal power and unique individuality; mutual help toward self-realization and self-sufficiency, etc.

162

Disturbed: Mutual inhibition of self-expression, self-realization and self-sufficiency; domination of one by the other; pressure from exaggerated ambition and demands; self-assertion at the expense of the partner; excessive lust for power; egocentricity, self-centeredness; recklessness; extreme competitiveness, etc.

Level 4 (Heart Chakra): The loving connectedness

In harmony: Warm, heartfelt affection; warmth, openness, trust and surrender; love which respects the other's freedom; deep bond without possessiveness; protectedness and inner peace; self-love; harmony with all through universal love; stillness; joy and inner harmony; receptiveness and vulnerability, etc.

Disturbed: Closed or broken heart; rejected love; fear and mistrust; isolation; lack of self-love; restlessness, etc.

Level 5 (Throat Chakra): Shared creativity and communication

In harmony: Support of individual or joint creative expression; mutual inspiration; mutual help through incentive and encouragement; open communication within the relationship and with other people; sharing inner wealth, etc.

Disturbed: Inhibition of creative expression; blockages in communication with the partner and others; lack of self-confidence; discouragement through negativity; underestimation of and disrespect for creative potential, etc.

Level 6 (Third Eye): Spiritual growth

In harmony: Spiritual bond; intuitive knowing; awareness; expanded perception; great empathy; clarity; knowing beyond words, etc.

Disturbed: Lack of trust in one's own perceptions; deep, dull feeling of senselessness; lack of openness to the »world beyond things«; restriction of and lack of respect for one's own spirituality; inability to see one's life from a higher perspective; cought in egocentric striving, etc.

Level 7 (Crown Chakra): The Relationship to the Whole

In harmony: Certainty of being cosmiconnected to the whole; transparency, permeability; openness for universal love and intelligence; experience of All-One-ness; harmony with the cosmic energies and forces, etc.

Disturbed: Lack of permeability and receptivity; experience of inner darkness and hopelessness; separation from the blessings of cosmic love; conscious or unconscious closedness to cosmic energies and forces, etc.

Brief Variation: Head – Heart – Sex

For this briefer version, draw one card for the head, one for the heart and one for the sexual connection to your partner. You can do this one together too. Start with the head, then the heart, end with sex. Use the following questions as a basis when you draw the cards.

Head: How do I harmonize with my partner on the level of the mind and intellectual exchange?

Heart: How do I harmonize with my partner on the level of heart's love, surrender, trust and heart connection?

Sex: How do I harmonize with my partner on the level of sexual and emotional satisfaction of needs?

First answer these questions to the best of your abilities, then draw a card for each one. Turn them over one by one and compare them with what you said. See where the differences lie.

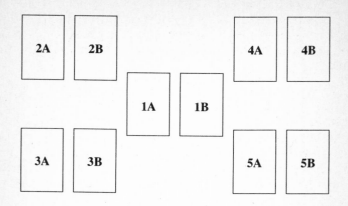

Layout 10

Relationship Karma

The meeting of two people which leads to a love relationship is never accidental. Your connection usually lies in the distant past established in earlier meetings. Present situations in a relationship are often repetitions or reversals of past events.

The degree to which we are able to recognize and appropriately solve the resulting lessons influences the degree to which we will experience joy or suffering, fulfillment or frustration.

This layout helps you to understand the present situation in connection to past and potential future karma.

You can use this system alone, or with your partner. The following description assumes that you are laying the cards together. You will take turns drawing cards until in all, ten have been drawn. If you are doing the layout alone, just draw five cards for yourself.

Sit next to each other, and tune in to your situation. Mix the cards and fan them out. Take turns drawing cards and laying them out in the pattern of Figure 6. Leave them face-down, and turn them up one by one.

Cards 1a and 1b show your deeper personal reality in the present situation. How are you really doing with your partner? What realms of your inner being are touched by your togetherness?

Cards 2a and 2b show the relationship from a cosmic viewpoint. These cards tell you what supreme lessons are to be learned by each partner in this relationship. What is most important for you to learn? What step toward greater consciousness are possible for you in this relationship?

Cards 3a and 3b show the karmic focus, or the main energy influencing your present situation which arises from the past. They tell you what karmic burdens or potentials are affecting your situation.

Cards 4a and 4b show how each of you is taking on the challenge of your relationship. What is your true behavior and attitude toward the current possibilities or problems? Are you bringing mostly openness and awareness, or fears and repressed energies into the relationship?

Cards 5a and 5b show what tendencies each partner is following in creating future karma. What the cards show for the future is never binding or guaranteed. It points out a general direction and expectation which carries a certain potential for realization within itself. Everyone has the opportunity and the freedom to change such tendencies. You can either improve them with love and awareness, or worsen them through lack of awareness and refusal.

7. The Relationship Card

The relationship card is determined through a combination of astrology and numerology. Numbers bear certain vibrations and symbolic energies. This makes it possible for us to calculate, using the birthdates of both partners, which card from the Major Arcana represents the shared purpose or the ultimate theme of a relationship. It shows the challenges, the tendencies, and the interplay of the two people.

The relationship card is determined in the following way:
- Add both birthdays (day, month, year).
- Add the digits of this sum to arrive at a new sum (for example, 3 + 9 + 5 + 3 = 20).
- Compare this number with the Major Arcana. 20 is The Aeon, your relationship card.
- If the second sum is greater than 22, add these two digits together again. For example, 3 + 9 + 5 + 6 = 23 and 2 + 3 = 5. The card numbered 5 is The Hierophant.
- If the second sum is exactly 22, your relationship card is The Fool. In the Egyptian Tarot, 22 is the same as 0, The Fool.

About the Author

Gerd Ziegler, born 2.8.51, has worked for many years as a therapist and trainer in the realm of humanistic and spiritual therapy. Even while studying psychology, political science, theatre education, and religion in Berlin, he was intensively involved with the areas of self-exploration and therapeutic work which were at that time relatively uncommon . He soon felt drawn to the schools which placed at the center of their education the interpersonal realms and holistic, spiritual growth.

Three sources were instrumental in inspiring him to recognize his path. They are the Initiation Therapy of Count Dürck-heim, the neoreichian bodywork of Gerda Boyesen, and, to an increasing degree, Bhagwan Shree Rajneesh who initiated him in 1979 and gave him the name Swami Bodhigyan.

In 1982 he founded the self-exploration and training project **Inwardly and Outwardly Rich** which rapidly gained participants from all German-speaking countries. The emphasis of this project is to open each person's gateway to the infinite potential within. There is great value in rediscovering this inner richness and expressing and sharing it in one's own life.

Gerd Ziegler uses Tarot as a medium to gain entrance into the inner depths of the consciousness. His Tarot classes are an intensive and lively introduction to the world of the Tarot and the various possibilities of using this medium of self-discovery for oneself and ohters.

Gerd Ziegler
is the initiator of the self-exploration
and training project

Inwardly and Outwardly Rich

Inner and outer richness describes a state of naturalness and boundless being, of unlimited surrender to oneself and life. The loss, search for, and rediscovery of this state of being is the process of our becoming conscious and complete.

Our work is not problem- but potential-oriented. We deal with problematic, painful, and fear-laden areas not as obstacles to be eliminated in the quickest possible way but as challenges and opportunities for transformation. In our fears, desires and passions slumber our greatest potentials. Even »problems« become valuable and important when we see them as hurdles making our path to liberation. They are like storms or trials which give roots to our being.

An important emphasis in the discovery and development of inner and outer richness is on **going beyond personal limits**. In our groups we constantly create situations in which people have the opportunity to step beyond their own boundaries. Such a step into expanded perception opens up new spaces inside which have a great effect on the searching process.

Our experience has shown again and again that every person who is determined to achieve self-realization already has all that is needed to facilitate physical, emotional, mental, and spiritual blossoming. This is what we call a person's inborn potential or inner richness.

The year-long training combines specific instruction with work on the individual growth process of each participant. The fundamental techniques and knowledge taught serve as a basis for any kind of work with people.

Information about the Tarot Courses or the training project **Inwardly and Outwardly Rich** can be obtained by writing to the address below. This is also the address for personal letters to Gerd Ziegler.

Gerd Ziegler, Regina König
Schulweg 4
D-8051 Zolling
West-Germany

8. Suggested Readings on the Theme »Relationships«

Allen, Marcus; **Tantra in the West**, New World Library, San Rafael CA, (formerly Whatever Publishing).

Bach, Richard; **Bridge Across Forever**, Ullstein, Berlin.

Gewain, Shakti; **Living in the Light**, New World Library.

Naslednikov, Margo; **Tantra – Way of Ecstasy**, Berlin.

Ray, Sondra; **Ja zur Liebe**, Peter Erd Verlag, 1987, (German Publisher).

Bhagwan Shree Rajneesh; **Love Comes After the Honeymoon**, Rajneesh-Services, Germany.

Bhagwan Shree Rajneesh; **Beziehungsdrama und Liebesabenteuer**, Rajneesh-Services, Germany.

Sagne, Cecile; **Geheiligter Eros**, Heyne Verlag, Munich 1987.

Robert Wang
Tarot Psychology

The Jungian Tarot opens the pathway to visualizing the diversity and variety of Jungian psychology. It represents a mosaic of pictures exactly related to each other and based on the terminology introduced by Jung in his method of »active imagination«. The goal is reaching a state of utter knowledge of the self. Jung has called this state »individuation«. On this stage of consciousness the true nature of life and death is understood.

The 78 drawings of the Jungian Tarot have been developed by Robert Wang as »archetypical pictures« – following Jung's conception of an interrelation between Tarot and the archetypes.

Robert Wang's work, his book on »Psychological Tarot« and the cards he created, represents a playful and easy-to-understand way of reaching Carl Gustav Jungs goal, i.e. absolute knowledge of the self.

Set (book + cards) ISBN 3-908647-02-9

ISBN 3-908647-01-0

Gerd Ziegler
Tarot – Mirror of the Soul

»In this pictures, the Crowley Thoth Tarot combines a wide variety of symbols and relates astrology, numerology and visualization to the symbolism of various schools of wisdom.«

Therefore, this Tarot system can become a comprehensive esoteric training and a source of deepest recognition for the user.

You are prepared for this by the detailed interpretation of the cards and their symbols. You will be fascinated by the intensive colours of this Tarot deck – sometimes archaically picturesque, sometimes artfully stylized. This deck has been designed following sketches of the famous esoteric master Aleister Crowley.

The deck has been published in this form for the first time in 1977. For this edition it has been newly reproduced from the original paintings.

ISBN 3-921960-43-6
Set (book + cards) ISBN 0-880793-22-8